To Pastor Seamogetswe Keoleletse my dear friend and fellow Kingdom worker

FATHER,
I NEED HELP

With love and respect

15/2/2024

FATHER, I NEED HELP

Our Father in Heaven is the LORD God almighty.
HE makes the impossible possible.

BOLA MAKINDE

FATHER, I NEED HELP

Copyright 2024 © Bola Makinde

ISBN: 9798877514201 (Paperback)
ISBN: 9798877514423 (Hardback)

Published by:
HFC Publications Limited
www.hfcpublications.com

HFC Publications Limited is the publishing arm of Heritage Foundation for Christ.

Scripture quotations are taken from NKJV, NIV and NLT.

Author's Note: Extensive Bible passages have been deliberately reproduced in this book. It was done for the specific reason of allowing readers in parts of the world where the Holy Bible may not be readily available, to have the full benefit of the many scriptures referenced in the book .

Book Designing and Assisted publishing by: manuscript2ebook.com

HE reverses the irreversible.
HE turns the natural into the supernatural;
and the ordinary into the extra-ordinary.
The LORD God almighty is our Father in Heaven.
There is absolutely none like HIM.

¹What shall we say, then? Shall we go on sinning so that grace may increase? ²By no means! We are those who have died to sin; how can we live in it any longer?

Romans 6:1-2

Prayer

I give all thanks, praises and adoration to our Father in Heaven, the LORD God almighty (El Shaddai) and His precious Son, our Lord Jesus Christ (Yeshua) for blessing me with the grace and enablement to write this book through the inspiration and empowerment of the Holy Spirit.

*I am confident that as you carefully read the pages and chapters of this book, the content will provide you with **spiritual nutrients** that will not only nurture your soul, but also help to expunge the **demonic toxins** that may have held you back in your Christian walk until now.*

*Every chapter contains a word, sentence or phrase that has the capacity to transform your soul, and help you to become the very best version of yourself in our Lord Jesus Christ. I call them **'believers nuggets'** and pray that you be generously blessed and highly favoured as you continue your Christian walk until eternity calls, in the mighty name of Jesus Christ, amen.*

Dedication

This book is dedicated to my wonderful late parents, Chief (Deacon) Gabriel Ekundayo Makinde and Mrs. Ebun Beatrice Makinde (nee Olayoku) for the singular fact that they allowed me to be born in spite of the risk to my beloved late mother's life.

May their blessed souls rest continuously and perpetually in peace in the mighty name of Jesus Christ, amen.

Special Acknowledgment

My dearest wife, Lola Makinde (nee Ogundipe) has been the one constant in my life for the past 32 years. She has demonstrated unusual tenacity to keep me going during the challenging years. The stability, steadfastness and continuity that her wisdom and counsel engendered during the good times meant that my life has enjoyed a balance that I could not have lived in any other way.

Acknowledgment and Thanks

If I have to thank everyone that has impacted my life positively at one stage or another, I will need several pages of this book to do so. There are just too many people that our LORD God almighty has used at various stages to direct me towards the right path whenever I have digressed from the primary purpose of my life.

Special thanks to Rev. Phil Robinson, Senior Minister at Whetstone Baptist Church in Leicester; Rev. Shaun Lambert, erstwhile Senior Minister at Stanmore Baptist Church in Harrow; late Rev (Dr.) Michael Carr and late Mrs. Patricia Carr, Founders of Harrow International Christian Centre (HICC); Pastor Paul James (erstwhile Senior Minister of (HICC); Dr. Albert Okoye (current Senior Minister of HICC) and his wife, Dr. Sylvia; my Brother-in-Law, Pastor Lekan Oludipe and his wife, Dr. Dupsy; Pastor Bola Ajidagba and his wife, Mrs. Tinuade Ajidagba of CAC Outreach Camberwell Church (It was from their weekly Bible Class that the Teaching Series that formed the basis of this book first started); Dr. Gboyega Martins (of Around the Globe with Dr. G on Sky TV, Ch. 66 or 582); Rev (Dr.) Peter Adegbie and his wife, Pastor Theodora of Chapel of Light International Church in Sunderland; Pastor Joseph Oluwatosin and his wife, Pastor Efe of RCCG House of Joy in Harrow; Bishop Ola David and his wife, Bishop Stella of Let the Earth Praise the Lord Ministries in Morden; Apostle Abayomi Olowo of The Gathering of the Saints Ministry in Ireland and his wife, Bola; Prophet Adebayo Odusanya a very kind friend in times of need; my very dear friend and mentor for over 26 years, late Mr. William Capstick and his wife, Celia; Dr. Tayo Olarewaju, my boss for several years; Mr. Mark Whitfield, my amazing Kingdom Brother in the Roman Catholic faith; Mr. Femi Alabi my encourager-in-chief and his wife, Remi; Princess Adejoke Adegoroye-Konu, my conscientious friend and Kingdom Sister; our very good friends of many years in HICC, Mr. Ope Opeodu (my President) and his wife, Anne; Mr. Layi Adeoye and his wife, Abbi; Mr. Isaac Negedu and his wife, Grace; Mr. Muyiwa Obileye and his wife, Bisola; Mr. Tunde Ogunade and his wife, Peju; Mr. Samson Oghene and his wife, Comfort; Mr. Abel Zea and his wife, Ruth; Mr. Tony Gilpin and his wife, Maxine; our very dear friends of many years based in the USA, Mr. Taiwo Adegoke and his wife, Modupe in Atlanta; Mr. Tony Aikhuele and his wife, Uche in New York and Mrs. Kemi Alli in Tampa, Florida; Miss Judith Brightwell, my loyal Assistant for many years; Dr. Folusho Falaye, my exceptional and indefatigable friend of over 40 years and his wife Lilian in Canada; Mr. Tunde Ajiniran for his daily prayers and encouragement; Mr. Ike Odina my dear friend and fellow Kingdom worker; my Uncle-in-Law, Mr. Abiodun Ogunsanwo and his wife, Mrs. Iyadunni Ogunsanwo; Mrs. Chilunji Dodwell my Kingdom Sister and friend from Zambia, Mr. Sailesraj Bala Murali, my young but impactful Kingdom Brother and friend from Malaysia; and finally Reverend Gbade Alabi of Free Will Baptist Church of Nigeria, my gentle mentor, encourager and amazing father-figure in Nigeria who graciously asked me one evening in my car at a Car Park somewhere in London 'Bola, with all these knowledge and giftings to teach that our LORD God almighty has poured into you, how can we take it to the world?' I actually did not know what to say in reply and probably mumbled something like 'at God's appointed time'. Though he may not realise it himself, our conversation of that night and his specific prayers for me; were actually the catalyst for this book. From the bottom of my heart, I thank him for his love and continuous fatherly encouragement.

As a matter of fact, you have all played key roles in my spiritual development at one time or another and for that, I am deeply and immensely grateful.

Table of Contents

Prologue

FATHER, I Need Help is for everyone, particularly believers in their journey of life. I use the word journey to describe our time on earth because it has a beginning and an end. One of the key questions that humans have pondered on since the beginning of creation is what happens when that journey ends. Some of the teachings in this book will address the question, though the primary aim of the book is how to make the most of what we do on the journey, rather than worrying about what happens after the end of the journey. In essence, if we do the right things on our journey of life, what happens at the end would not matter that much, as it would take care of itself. The one assurance that believers have if they have lived that journey well is their home in Heaven.

[1]"Let not your heart be troubled; you believe in God, believe also in me. [2]In my Father's house are many mansions; if it were not so, I would have told you. I go to prepare a place for you. [3]And if I go and prepare a place for you, I will come again and receive you to myself; that where I am, there you may be also".

John 14: 1-3

Introduction

¹⁵I do not understand what I do. For what I want to do I do not do, but what I hate I do.

¹⁶And if I do what I do not want to do, I agree that the law is good. ¹⁷As it is, it is no longer I myself who do it, but it is sin living in me. ¹⁸For I know that good itself does not dwell in me, that is, in my sinful nature. For I have the desire to do what is good, but I cannot carry it out.

¹⁹For I do not do the good I want to do, but the evil I do not want to do—this I keep on doing. ²⁰Now if I do what I do not want to do, it is no longer I who do it, but it is sin living in me that does it. ²¹So I find this law at work: Although I want to do good, evil is right there with me.

²²For in my inner being I delight in God's law; ²³but I see another law at work in me, waging war against the law of my mind and making me a prisoner of the law of sin at work within me. ²⁴What a wretched man I am! Who will rescue me from this body that is subject to death?

²⁵Thanks be to God, who delivers me through Jesus Christ our Lord!

Romans 7: 15-25

For the most part of my life and now a little after six decades, I have thought that I understood the things of God. Over the years, I have read the Bible regularly, prayed regularly, fasted regularly, and given generously to the best of my knowledge, understanding, and financial ability. Despite several challenges that included a life threatening illness that required two surgeries (one of which was major), almost complete loss of business ventures and the capacity to earn income, and struggles at home with spouse and children, I never stopped believing in our LORD God almighty and His Son Jesus Christ. I wrote sermons, preached in churches, counselled many people with results that included life transforming testimonies. In spite of all these experiences, I knew deep down that something was missing because I struggled with pride, arrogance, and pomposity during the good times. When the hard times came, I became bitter and resentful as I struggled with envy, jealousy, and deep insecurities. At different times, I also had issues with anxieties, fear, and even depression. Quite interestingly, I also struggled with lust, negative thoughts, and unforgiveness.

What intrigued me most was that throughout these periods, I attended church services regularly, served actively in church in various capacities which included ushering, discipleship leader, and even as an area pastor.

Things got to a peak and then one morning whilst on my knees praying, I said to myself that something is not right and for the first time I asked our Father in Heaven for help. In essence, my cry that morning was, 'FATHER, I NEED HELP'.

I continued praying the same prayer for a period of three days, asking our Father in Heaven **to deliver me from me,** as it became obvious that I was the problem and not anyone around me. Not my wife, not my daughter, not my son, not members of my extended family, not my friends, and definitely not anybody connected to me. In essence, I was the problem. **Something within my soul (my inner man) struggled with yielding to the Holy Spirit and dying to self, which is a prerequisite for true Kingdom living on earth.** Hence, my prayer request to our LORD God almighty, our Father in Heaven was to have mercy on me and **save me from me**.

After three days of praying the same prayer, the answer arrived; like I was in a dark room and someone came into the room and simply switched on the light. Suddenly, I could see things clearly and was able to understand my circumstances without any equivocation or confusion. It was as if a mighty burden was lifted off my shoulder. Anger, resentment, bitterness, envy, jealousy, arrogance, pride, anxiety, fear, lust, unforgiveness, etc. left me all at once. I was delivered from all kinds of bondages and insecurities that had bogged my life over many years.

Shortly afterwards, I registered a Christian Foundation, aptly named Heritage Foundation for Christ. Not long after, the Teaching Series started. It actually came from an inspiration from the Holy Spirit as I was deliberating in my mind as to what to do with the Foundation. Prior to that time, I joined a Bible Class that was led by another Kingdom Brother and his wife, where I was asked to teach occasionally. The Holy Spirit instructed me in clear language to start sharing the Teaching Series with family and friends. I started with those on my phone's contact list.

The rest, as they say, is history.

CHAPTER 1

You will seek Me

*¹³You will seek Me and find Me when you **seek** Me with all your heart.*

Over the years, I have had the privilege of speaking to many of our Christian brothers and sisters about prayers, what we pray for, and our relationship with our LORD God almighty, His Son Jesus Christ, and the Holy Spirit. Often I have come away **wondering what our priorities** are as Christians.

Many times, I have watched Christian programmes on the television and listened with concern to what is being preached. What appears to me as the common trend is, the focus of many of the teachers on prosperity, breakthroughs, finance, success, healing, miracles, etc. Hardly does anyone talk as much about the Holy Spirit, about salvation, about eternity, about hell, etc. I can hardly remember the last time I heard anyone preach extensively about heaven or about paradise or what comes next after life.

A lot of people focus on the 'asking' as taught by our Lord Jesus Christ in Matthew 7: 7, but how many people understand the fact that true and eternal blessings come from 'seeking' and **finding** God.

*⁷Ask and it will be given to you; **seek and you will find**; knock and the door will be opened to you.*

7

When we seek God with all our heart, the passage in *Jeremiah 29: 13* clearly shows that we will find Him. Sometimes people ask me, 'How else does one seek God apart from coming to church regularly?' My answer is simple. Yes, you can seek God by coming to church regularly, and added to that, by reading your Bible regularly; meditating continuously on the Word of God; fasting and more importantly living a life of holiness and righteousness in obedience to the commands of our LORD God almighty and His Son Jesus Christ.

You see, when we focus on our **needs** and **wants** continuously in prayer, we are simply focusing on the **carrots** of life. When we focus on prosperity, breakthroughs, finance, success, healing, miracles, etc., we are simply focusing on the carrots which do not help us on the path to eternal life with our LORD God almighty.

Now, let us see what our Lord Jesus Christ has to say about the carrots of life.

*24 No one can serve two masters. Either you will hate the one and love the other, or you will be devoted to the one and despise the other. **You cannot serve both God and money**. 25Therefore I tell you, **do not worry** about your life, what you will eat or what you will drink; or about your body, what you will wear. Is not life more important than food, and the body more important than clothes? 26Look at the birds of the air, they do not sow or reap or store away in barns, and yet your heavenly Father feeds them. Are you not **much more valuable** than they? 27Who of you by worrying can add a single hour to his life?*

Matthew 6: 24-27

*31So **do not worry**, saying, 'What shall we eat?' or 'What shall we drink?' or 'What shall we wear?' 32For the pagans run after all these things, and your heavenly Father knows that you need them. 33But **seek** first the kingdom of God and **His righteousness** and all these things shall be given to you as well.*

Matthew 6: 31-33

Verse 33 makes it clear that we are to seek our LORD God almighty and His righteousness first. When we do that, we are seeking the **Carrot Giver**. The implication of seeking the Carrot Giver is that, not only will you have the Carrot, but you will also have the Giver of the Carrot as well. Hence, when we seek God first and His **righteousness**, most of the things we seek will come to us and we will not have to chase them as they shall be added to us, even when we have not asked for them. **Besides, our focus will change, because we will no longer seek God for our wants and other selfish reasons, instead we will seek God to worship and serve Him in spirit and truth *(John 4: 23)*.** And yes, we will go from breakthroughs to breakovers.

Moreover, the blessings that come with seeking and finding our LORD God almighty will be channelled towards Kingdom service. **When you seek God with all your heart and find Him, you will discover that your focus changes from self-interest to God-interest and Kingdom matters i.e. Kingdom promotion; Kingdom welfare; Kingdom elevation; and Kingdom expansion.**

This is because with blessings, comes responsibility and the realisation that when you seek God first and His righteousness, you will be a channel of blessing when it comes to winning souls for our Lord Jesus Christ, populating Heaven and plundering Hell. Yes, you will partake in bringing salvation to many homes and deliverance to many families and our LORD God almighty will take all the glory in the mighty name of Jesus Christ, amen.

After all said and done, perhaps the greatest blessing that comes with seeking our LORD God almighty with all our heart and finding Him is **the transformative gift of the Holy Spirit that we receive from God,** as demonstrated in *Romans 8.*

[10]But if Christ is in you, then even though your body is subject to death because of sin, the Spirit gives life because of righteousness. [11]And if the Spirit of Him

who raised Jesus from the dead is living in you, He who raised Christ from the dead will also give life to your mortal bodies because of His Spirit who lives in you. **¹²Therefore, brothers and sisters, we have an obligation—but it is not to the flesh, to live according to it.** *¹³For if you live according to the flesh, you will die; but if by the Spirit you put to death the misdeeds of the body, you will live.* **¹⁴For those who are led by the Spirit of God are the children of God.**

Romans 8: 10-14

CHAPTER 2

From Bondage
to Empowerment

Four Steps to Salvation

1. Bondage
2. Stronghold
3. Deliverance
4. Empowerment

Bondage

When people are in bondage, in most cases, they would not be aware that they are in bondage, which in essence makes it difficult for them to acknowledge that they are in bondage.

What is bondage in the Christian parlance? It can take different forms or come in different shapes. For example, some people are always sad for no apparent reason. They never smile and every little thing irritates them. In most cases and particularly because they are not contented with what they have, they are unhappy because of the things they lack instead of being happy for the things they already have. It is similar to seeing your cup of life as half empty instead of seeing it as half full.

¹²*I know what it is to be in need, and I know what it is to have plenty. I have learned the secret of being content in any and every situation, whether well*

fed or hungry, whether living in plenty or in want. ¹³*I can do all this through Him who gives me strength.*

Philippians 4 :12-13

Another example of bondage is bitterness and lack of forgiveness. Some people just simply refuse to forgive and it becomes an albatross on their necks. In the process, their lack of forgiveness takes away their joy and peace.

¹⁴*For if you forgive other people when they sin against you, your Heavenly Father will also forgive you.* ¹⁵*But if you do not forgive others their sins, your Father will not forgive your sins.*

Matthew 6: 14-15

Bondage can also come in the shape of resentment or envy or jealousy of a friend or family member to the extent that when that person comes into your presence, your heartbeat does a double take or you start having palpitations as if you are having a panic attack. In short, you simply detest the fellow and find it difficult to have him or her around you; not to talk of loving the person as our Lord Jesus Christ instructs us to do, as well as Peter in **1 Peter 4: 8.**

⁸*Above all, love each other deeply, because love covers over a multitude of sins.*

1 Peter 4: 8

Bondage is a demonic spirit and it attacks the mind. The spirit of bondage is also a weakening spirit. It does not empower you in any shape or form, hence the scripture says you should capture negative and evil thoughts and instead think as advised by Paul in his writing to the Philippians:

⁸*Finally, brothers and sisters, whatever is true, whatever is noble, whatever is right, whatever is pure, whatever is lovely, whatever is admirable—if anything is excellent or praiseworthy—think about such things.*

Philippians 4: 8

Other forms of bondages can be seen in acts of pride, wickedness, smoking, stealing, fornication, adultery, kleptomania, drug addiction, as well as all other types of addictions, which includes watching pornography and mendacious actions, amongst others. These are all manifestations of a person gripped by the demonic spirit of bondage.

19 The acts of the flesh are obvious: sexual immorality, impurity and debauchery; 20 idolatry and witchcraft; hatred, discord, jealousy, fits of rage, selfish ambition, dissensions, factions 21 and envy; drunkenness, orgies, and the like.

Galatians 5: 19-21

When a person is in bondage, it is most likely that such a person will be in denial with respect to the consequences of the problem they are facing and may not seek help. Such people may even think that they are enjoying their lives and that there is nothing wrong with what they are doing. Some of them will even misquote the Bible for you and merely say that there is no condemnation for those in Christ Jesus, which is a mistaken position to be in **(Romans 8: 1)**. Paul dealt with this point in **Roman 6: 1-2** when he wrote, 'What shall we say, then? Shall we go on sinning, so that grace may increase? By no means! We died to sin; how can we live in it any longer'.

1Therefore, there is now no condemnation for those who are in Christ Jesus,

Romans 8: 1

The one common thread of people still caught up in bondage is the absence of the **fear of God**. Sometimes, a person in bondage could actually be a regular church goer and even love our Lord Jesus Christ, but still thinks that he or she can engage in actions that are obviously sinful and thereafter simply pray for forgiveness. The only thing that stops people from deliberately living in sin or engaging in sinful acts, is the genuine fear of our LORD God almighty.

¹⁰The fear of the LORD is the beginning of wisdom, and knowledge of the Holy one is understanding. ¹¹For through wisdom your days will be many, and years will be added to your life.

Proverbs 9:10-11

Stronghold

A by-product of being held in bondage is facing a stronghold. At this stage, the person in bondage has realised that he has a problem, but unfortunately the problem has such a strong hold on him that he is struggling to break free. This is common amongst people with addictions like hard drugs, alcohol abuse, smoking, adultery, pornography, etc. Though they are now aware that their addiction is causing them serious problems, unfortunately they just cannot get out of it or free themselves from their problems.

The key question at this stage is how does one deal with people in this situation? Those in the medical profession often have various remedies to offer people facing strongholds. In most cases, their remedies result in temporary relief and after a while, the victims go back to their old ways, which is called 'relapse'.

The Word of God says that though we are in the world, but we are not of the world. For those who believe in God, the solution for such problems is to resort to prayers and fasting, because the actual root cause of the problems faced by people in bondages and those facing strongholds is spiritual *(because we are also spirit beings)*, which then becomes manifested in the physical **(Mark 9: 28-29)**. Because the root cause of their problem is spiritual, the approach to dealing with it in order to have a permanent solution has to be spiritual, which will then become manifested in the physical well-being of the victim. You see, in **1 Peter 5: 8**, the devil is described as a roaring lion looking for whom to devour. It is my prayer that we and our families never become one of his victims in the mighty name of Jesus Christ, amen.

[28] And when He had come into the house, His disciples asked Him privately, "Why could we not cast it out?" [29] So he said to them, 'This kind can come out by nothing but prayer and fasting'.

Mark 9: 28-29

[8] Be alert and of sober mind. Your enemy the devil prowls around like a roaring lion looking for someone to devour.

1 Peter 5: 8

Deliverance

Deliverance comes when a person gives his or her life to our Lord Jesus Christ. This can happen in a church setting or in a gathering where prayers are being offered for the purpose of deliverance or even in your own home through praying fervently privately by yourself as was the case with me. The Word of God says that when a person gives his life to Christ, all things are passed away and that the person becomes a new creature in Christ. Our Lord Jesus Christ taught us in **Matthew 11: 28-29** as follows.

*[28] Come to me, all you who are weary and burdened, and I will give you rest. [29] Take my yoke upon you and learn from me, for I am gentle and humble in heart, and **you will find rest for your souls**. [30] For my yoke is easy and my burden is light.*

Matthew 11: 28-30

One key ingredient of deliverance is the need for **repentance (Matthew 3: 1-2)**. 'Create in me a pure heart, O God, and renew a steadfast spirit within me', David wrote in **Psalm 51**. He went further in verses 11 and 12.

*[1] In those days John the Baptist came, preaching in the wilderness of Judea [2] and saying, "**Repent**, for the kingdom of heaven has come near."*

Matthew 3: 1-2

[11] Do not cast me from your presence or take your Holy Spirit from me. [12] Restore to me the joy of your salvation and grant me a willing spirit, to sustain me.

Psalm 51: 11-12

At this stage, a person experiences a renewal of his/her mind, which explains why Paul reiterated in **Roman 12:2** when he wrote, 'Do not conform any longer to the pattern of this world, but be transformed by the renewing of your mind'.

To enjoy an effective deliverance, a person must make a firm decision to give his/her life to our Lord Jesus Christ by yielding to the **Holy Spirit,** which then enables the person to resist the devil, because they are not doing it by their own power, but with the enablement of the Holy Spirit.

[2] Do not conform to the pattern of this world, but be transformed by the renewing of your mind. Then you will be able to test and approve what God's will is—his good, pleasing and perfect will.

Roman 12: 2

The mistake some people make however at this stage is to assume that now that they are born again, they can live a life that is free of problems and that everything will be hunky-dory henceforth. Unfortunately, without the Holy Spirit's empowerment and His continuous indwelling presence in a person, he/she will not be completely free from their old ways and will sooner or later backslide.

Empowerment

The Word of God says in **Zechariah 4: 6**, it is not by might or by power, but by my spirit. Prior to our Lord Jesus Christ departing this world, He promised to send the Holy Spirit to His disciples (**Acts 1: 4-5, Acts 1: 8**). Shortly after the crucifixion, most of the disciples were already discouraged to see their Messiah on the cross, but the resurrection of our Lord Jesus Christ and the visitation of the Holy Spirit at Pentecost changed everything.

*[6] So he said to me, "This is the word of the Lord to Zerubbabel: 'Not by might nor by power, **but by my Spirit**,' says the Lord Almighty."*

Zechariah 4: 6

[4] On one occasion, while he was eating with them, he gave them this command: "Do not leave Jerusalem, but wait for the gift my Father promised, which you have heard me speak about. [5] For John baptized with water, but in a few days you will be baptized with the Holy Spirit."

Acts 1: 4-5

*[8] **But you will receive power when the Holy Spirit comes on you**; and you will be my witnesses in Jerusalem, and in all Judea and Samaria, and to the ends of the earth.*

Acts 1: 8

It is only through the empowerment of the Holy Spirit that a person can truly resist the devil and then the devil flees from him/her *(James 4:7)*. Without yielding to the Holy Spirit, a person cannot resist the devil by his/her own power and the devil will not flee from him/her. But when you are filled with the Holy Spirit and the devil sees that you are surrounded by a host of Angels and fully covered by the Holy Spirit, he will flee from you as quickly as possible and without hesitation.

[7] Submit yourselves, then, to God. Resist the devil, and he will flee from you.

James 4: 7

The irony is that most believers today operate between the stages of Stronghold and Deliverance, thus alternating between the two stages for the most part of their lives without moving permanently to the Empowerment stage.

The result is that they are not productive Christians and are also without the power that is fuelled by the Holy Spirit, which is needed in order to confront and overcome the enemy (devil). Sadly and quite sadly, they end up as defeated Christians, instead of victorious Christians.

In essence, it is the continuous indwelling presence and empowerment of the Holy Spirit in a person that prevents him/her, not only from going back to their old ways, but puts them into a position where they begin to experience the joy of salvation in Jesus Christ, and also become effective witnesses for Christ, in the process yielding souls for the Kingdom of God by populating Heaven and plundering Hell.

When you become filled with the Holy Spirit as a believer, the realisation takes away the fear to witness and replaces it with the courage and wisdom to be the true and effective light of the world and salt of the earth (*Matthew 5:13-14*).

13"You are the salt of the earth. But if the salt loses its saltiness, how can it be made salty again? It is no longer good for anything, except to be thrown out and trampled underfoot. 14 You are the light of the world. A town built on a hill cannot be hidden."

<u>*Matthew 5: 13-14*</u>

CHAPTER 3

Beacons for Holy Living

It starts with two key questions:

1. **Are you yielded?**

2. **Do you abide?**

If you are unable to answer both questions in the affirmative, then you need to ask deep questions about the direction of your Christian life.

Are You Yielded?

What does it mean for a believer to be yielded? Another way that the question can be framed is, are you yielded and already enjoying the fruits of the Holy Spirit? (*Galatians 5:22-23*); Or does your relationship with our LORD God almighty allow you to approach Him with confidence? (*1John 5: 14-15*); Or have you submitted yourself to God and as such empowered to resist the devil? (*James 4: 7*); Or do you still worship God with just your lips, but not with your heart? (*Isaiah 29: 13*); Or are you hot, cold, or lukewarm in your Christian walk? (*Rev. 3: 15-16*); Or have you died to self? (*Matthew 16: 24-26*); Or are you born again or just a good regular church goer? (*John 3: 3*)

Let us look at what the scriptures say

²²But the fruit of the Spirit is love, joy, peace, forbearance, kindness, goodness, faithfulness, ²³gentleness and self-control. Against such things there is no law.

Galatians 5: 22-23

*¹⁴ This is the confidence that we have in approaching God: that if we ask anything according to **His will, He hears us**. ¹⁵And if we know that He hears us—whatever we ask—we know that we have what we asked of Him.*

1 John 5: 14-15

¹³The Lord says: "These people come near to me with their mouth and honour me with their lips, but their hearts are far from me. Their worship of me is based on merely human rules they have been taught.

Isaiah 29: 13

¹⁵I know your deeds, that you are neither cold nor hot. I wish you were either one or the other! ¹⁶ So, because you are lukewarm—neither hot nor cold—I am about to spit you out of my mouth.

Revelations 3: 15-16

*²⁴Then Jesus said to his disciples, "Whoever wants to be my disciple must deny themselves and take up their cross and follow me. ²⁵For whoever wants to save their life will lose it, but whoever loses their life for me will find it. ²⁶What good will it be for someone to gain the whole world, yet forfeit their **soul**? Or what can anyone give in exchange for their **soul**?*

Matthew 16: 24-26

³Jesus answered and said unto him, 'Verily, verily, I say unto thee. Except a man be born again, he cannot see the kingdom of God.

John 3: 3

Do You Abide?

It is often said that the Christian life is about freedom in Christ and a life of abundance and prosperity. Yes, that is all well and good. The other more important point about the Christian life is that it is also a life of sacrifice that involves denying yourself activities that gratify your sinful flesh. This is actually the crux of victorious Christian living. The requirement to **obey** (*Luke 6: 46, Samuel 15: 22-23*) and **abide** (*Luke 11: 27-28*) is one of the most difficult requirements of Christian living. The words **"obey"** and **"abide"** (*Matthew 7:21-27*) **challenge every believer because it is the very antithesis of our nature and humanity**.

The human nature instinctively wants to gratify the sinful flesh and this happens in many ways starting with petty lies, which progresses to embellishments of stories, and then graduates to cheating, lustfulness, fornication, adultery, and all other kinds of sins that result in everything that opposes a life of **holiness** and **righteousness**.

Let us look at what the scriptures say

*⁴⁶"Why do you call me, 'LORD, LORD,' and **do not do** what I say?"*

Luke 6: 46

*²⁷As Jesus was saying these things, a woman in the crowd called out, "Blessed is the mother who gave you birth and nursed you." ²⁸He replied, "Blessed rather are those who hear the word of God and **obey** it."*

Luke 11: 27-28

*²¹ "Not everyone who says to me, 'Lord, Lord,' will enter the kingdom of heaven, but only the one who does the will of my Father who is in heaven. ²² Many will say to me on that day, 'Lord, Lord, did we not prophesy in your name and in your name drive out demons and in your name perform many miracles?' ²³ Then I will tell them plainly, 'I never knew you. Away from me, you evildoers!' ²⁴**Therefore everyone who hears these words of mine and puts them into practice is like a wise man who built his house on the rock**. ²⁵ The rain came down, the streams rose, and the winds blew and beat against that house; yet it did not fall, because it had its foundation on the rock. ²⁶But everyone who hears these words of mine and does not put them* *into practice is like a foolish man who built his house on sand. ²⁷The rain came down, the streams rose, and the winds blew and beat against that house, and it fell with a great crash."*

Matthew 7: 21-27

The Answer

Quite simple. It is the **Holy Spirit**.

In these end times, the body of Christ needs to know and understand more about the Holy Spirit and particularly His role as our **HELPER (***John 14: 15-17***)** and our **GUIDE (***John 16: 13-14***). His indwelling presence in our lives is similar to having the very presence of our LORD God almighty residing in us as He helps us to remain obedient to the teachings of our Lord Jesus Christ (***Luke 6:46***)**, which then results in a life that is truly yielded (***James 4: 7***) and also able to abide (***John 15: 7-8***).

Otherwise, **the very idea of trying to live the Christian life without being filled and empowered by the Holy Spirit is like trying to build a house without first digging the foundation.** The type of Christians that our human efforts and carnal minds produce are the ones that line up in front of church on Sundays and wait for someone with a "special anointing" to lay hands on them and thereafter expect all their problems to be solved, whereas what they actually need is to yield to God and be filled and empowered by the Holy Spirit, so that they can abide and as such be able to live the victorious Christian life 24/7.

*¹⁵ "If you love me, keep my commands. ¹⁶And I will ask the Father, and he will give you **another advocate** to help you and be with you forever— ¹⁷the **Spirit of truth**. The world cannot accept him, because it neither sees him nor knows him. But you know him, for he lives with you and will be in you. ... ²¹ **Whoever has my commands and keeps them is the one who loves me.***

*The one who loves me will be loved by my Father, and I too will love them and **show myself** to them."*

John 14: 15-17, 21

*[13] But when He, the **Spirit of truth**, comes, He will **guide** you into all the truth. He will not speak on his own; He will speak only what He hears, and He will tell you what is yet to come. [14] He will glorify me because it is from me that He will receive what He will make known to you.*

John 16: 13-14

*[7]**If you remain in me and my words remain in you, ask whatever you wish, and it will be done for you**. [8] This is to my Father's glory, that you bear much fruit, showing yourselves to be my disciples.*

John 15: 7-8

In order to **crystallise our life in Christ**, it is essential to start eating the solid food of teachings on **holiness** and **righteousness** instead of the milk of performance and entertainment that is sometimes served on some pulpits (not all) and TV channels in different parts of the world, which only serves to excite our sinful flesh and probably nothing more. It explains why our lifestyles do not change, which then results in zero impact on the people around us, either in our homes, offices, families or amongst our friends.

However, in order to truly begin to experience the Power of God in all its fullness without needing an intermediary between you and our LORD God almighty, you need to make a **personal commitment** to seek our LORD God almighty with all your heart (*Jeremiah 29:13*) because what you seek is what you find.

The **beacons for holy living** are simple to embrace, and the good news is that with the **help** of the **Holy Spirit**, doing so comes with being rewarded with a life that is filled to the measure of all the fulness of our LORD God almighty whilst still on planet earth

(*Ephesians 3: 14-19*) and followed by eternity with our Lord Jesus Christ when our time on earth comes to an end.

CHAPTER 4

'... but by my Spirit'

Shortly after returning to my hotel sometime in February, 2017 after attending a business meeting in China, I was so perplexed and demoralised because of what transpired at the end of the meeting, which went against all my expectations. Quite interestingly, the meeting started very well and almost all the expected boxes were being ticked. Everyone seemed happy until towards the end when a couple of unexpected demands were made by my hosts, which sadly no one mentioned to me before I departed London for Guiyang, China.

Because the outcome of the meeting was so depressing, on getting back to the hotel I got under the duvet cover fully clothed, without even taking off my shoes. I wondered in despair how it all happened, and how on earth I found myself in that situation. I questioned myself as to the quality of the due diligence that could have been done to ensure that no stone was left unturned before I departed the United Kingdom for China.

It was at that moment I realised why some people do stupid things when they are at the end of their tether. Despite having left the meeting with a signed contract in my hand, I knew that the signed contract meant nothing unless the conditions attached to them were fulfilled, which to all intent and purposes were next to almost impossible as they involved additional financial costs on my part. Sadly, without my having the funds to fulfil them at the time, it was a non-starter on my part. I remained in that state of anxiety, disappointment, and sadness for several minutes, following which I then decided to pick up my Bible and opened it randomly to read. Your guess is as good as mine as to the page that I opened to read.

The Book of Zechariah 4: 6-7

⁶*So he said to me, "This is the word of the Lord to Zerubbabel: '**Not by might, nor by power, but by my spirit**,' says the Lord Almighty.* ⁷*"What are you, mighty mountain? Before Zerubbabel you will become level ground. Then he will bring out the capstone to shouts of 'God bless it! God bless it!'"*

After reading the Bible for a while, I slept off for what felt like a few hours, only to be woken up by a phone call from a business colleague in London—an Executive Director of one of my companies at the time who gave me some wonderful news about the contract he had just signed on our behalf. He continued to say that everything was going to be okay, without having any idea of what transpired at the meeting I had a few hours earlier. How ironic. Just as one door closed, another bigger and better one opened. **Now you can understand why you should not do anything stupid when things do not go well for you, as in all things our LORD God almighty works for the good of those who love Him and who have been called according to His purpose (*Romans 8: 28*).**

At the time of these events in 2017, I did not know or understand the full implications of what just transpired. The implications of '*... but by my Spirit.*' I am not alone as this is one of the most **significant aspects of our Christian walk that is often missed**, even by great men of God as well as accomplished Bible teachers who dedicate all their lives to the Christian ministry. The key word in what is often missed is **revelation**. In simple terms, unless the meanings of the Word of our LORD God almighty and the teachings of our Lord

Jesus Christ are **revealed** to you by the **Holy Spirit**, it is an exercise in futility as all you will have is lots of head knowledge of the Word of God, which naturally breeds pride and arrogance about knowing the Word, but nothing more.

One important thing that I did before embarking on my trip to China was to ask the Pastor to pray for me. Pastor Paul James, the Senior Minister at Harrow International Christian Centre (HICC) at the time, laid his hands on me and prayed fervently for a safe and blessed trip. I can say categorically that our LORD God almighty answered his prayers as three specific things happened on the trip.

Firstly, at Guangzhou Airport during my transfer to Guiyang, as I disembarked from the plane to transfer to my connecting flight, I spotted a flight attendant holding a sign with my name. She informed me of the altered arrangements and advised me to retrieve my baggage and re-check it in for the flight to Guiyang, (I could easily have overlooked her).

Secondly, it was the manner in which our God almighty revealed Himself to me through His words when I was at the end of my tether in my hotel room after a disappointing meeting.

Thirdly, on the return leg of my trip, I mistakenly left my debit cards and credit cards on the check-in desk after checking-in at Beijing Airport. Just as I was about to proceed to the Departures lounge, I saw one of the ladies that attended to me earlier with a distressed look as she appeared to be looking frantically for someone. Alas, I did not realise that I was the person she was looking for and when she saw me, there was a huge sigh of relief on her face as she returned my credit cards and debit cards to me. The irony was that I did not even realise that I had mistakenly dropped them whilst checking-in at her desk. What can I say, we serve an amazing FATHER who looks after us and continues to work on our behalf even when we don't know about it. He is truly our **El Shaddai—our Father in Heaven who does for us the things that we cannot do ourselves.**

I am going to use the next few paragraphs and Bible passages to shine some light on the focal point that this chapter aims to address. Hopefully, every person that reads this book will develop an understanding of why **even our Lord Jesus Christ needed to operate with the help of the Holy Spirit** when He walked on planet earth and particularly when He was confronted by the devil.

*¹Jesus, **full of the Holy Spirit**, left the Jordan and was led by the **Spirit** into the wilderness, ²where for forty days he was tempted by the devil. He ate nothing during those days, and at the end of them he was hungry. ³The devil said to him, "If you are the Son of God, tell this stone to become bread." ⁴Jesus answered, "It is written: 'Man shall not live on bread alone.'"*

⁵The devil led him up to a high place and showed him in an instant all the kingdoms of the world. ⁶And he said to him, "I will give you all their authority and splendour; it has been given to me, and I can give it to anyone I want to. ⁷If you worship me, it will all be yours." ⁸Jesus answered, "It is written: 'Worship the LORD your God and serve Him only.'" ⁹The devil led him to Jerusalem and had him stand on the highest point of the temple. "If you are the Son of God," he said, "throw yourself down from here. ¹⁰For it is written: 'He will command His angels concerning you to guard you carefully; ¹¹they will lift you up in their hands, so that you will not strike your foot against a stone.'" ¹²Jesus answered, "It is said: 'Do not put the Lord your God to the test.'"

Luke 4: 1-12

As it is evident from the above scripture, even our Lord Jesus Christ needed to be full of the *Holy Spirit* in order to overcome the devil when he was tempted. Often times, we make the mistake that just because we know the Bible and can quote several passages or have the ability to pray all night, we reckon that we are equipped to overcome the devil and his demonic emissaries. Sadly, from what I understand now, it is not that simple. Now consider what our Lord Jesus Christ told his disciples before He left them after He rose from the death.

*⁴⁹I am going to send you what my Father has promised; but stay in the city until you have been clothed with **power** from on high."*

Luke 24: 49

This was repeated on more occasions in the **Book of Acts** by our Lord Jesus Christ:

*⁴On one occasion, while he was eating with them, he gave them this command: "Do not leave Jerusalem, but wait for the **gift** my Father promised, which you have heard me speak about. ⁵For John baptized with water, but in a few days you will be baptized with the **Holy Spirit**."*

Acts1: 4-5

*"And you shall receive **power** when the **Holy Spirit** has come upon you; and you shall be my witnesses in Jerusalem and in all Judea and Samaria and to the end of the earth."*

Acts 1: 8

*We are witnesses of these things, and so is the **Holy Spirit**, whom God has given to those who **obey** him.*

Acts 5: 32

Apostle Paul also needed to be filled with the Holy Spirit before he could start his ministry as shown in the passage below.

*¹⁷Then Ananias went to the house and entered it. Placing his hands on Saul, he said, "Brother Saul, the Lord—Jesus, who appeared to you on the road as you were coming here—has sent me so that you may see again **and be filled with the Holy Spirit**." ¹⁸Immediately, something like scales fell from Saul's eyes, and he could see again. He got up and was baptized,...*

Acts 9: 17-18

Revelation

It is the **Holy Spirit** that **reveals** the meanings of the messages in the Word of our LORD God almighty as the holy Bible is not just about the stories. Every story and every message in the holy Bible has spiritual implications. That is why when you give your life to our Lord Jesus Christ, it is imperative that you pray specifically to be **filtered, filled,** and **empowered** by the **Holy Spirit** so that you can live your Christian life in a manner that is consistent with the commandments of our Lord Jesus Christ on holiness and righteousness.

*¹⁵ "If you love me, keep my commands. ¹⁶And I will ask the Father, and **he will give you another advocate to help you and be with you forever**— ¹⁷the Spirit of truth. The world cannot accept him, because it neither sees him nor knows him. But you know him, for he lives with you and will be in you. ¹⁸I will not leave you as orphans; I will come to you. ¹⁹Before long, the world will not see me anymore, but you will see me. Because I live, you also will live. ²⁰On that day you will realize that I am in my Father, and you are in me, and I am in you. ²¹Whoever has my commands and keeps them is the one who loves me. The one who loves me will be loved by my father, and I too will love them and show (reveal) Myself to them." ²²Then Judas (not Judas Iscariot) said, "But, Lord, why do you intend to show yourself to us and not to the world?" ²³Jesus replied, "Anyone who loves me will obey my teaching. My Father will love them, and we will come to them and make our home with them. ²⁴Anyone who does not love me will not obey my teaching. These words you hear are not my own; they belong to the Father who sent me.*

John 14: 15-24

Paul expanded on this theme in the book of Corinthians when he wrote extensively on **wisdom** from the **Spirit**. I suggest that you prayerfully read the passages below and deduce for yourself the depth of the importance of the **Holy Spirit** in your Christian walk.

¹⁵ For this reason, ever since I heard about your faith in the Lord Jesus and your love for all God's people, ¹⁶ I have not stopped giving thanks for you, *remembering you in my prayers. ¹⁷I keep asking that the God of our Lord Jesus Christ, the glorious Father, may give you the **Spirit** of **wisdom** and **revelation**, so that you may know him better.*

Ephesians 1: 15-17

*⁶We do, however, speak a message of wisdom among the mature, but not the wisdom of this age or of the rulers of this age, who are coming to nothing. ⁷No, we speak of God's secret wisdom, a wisdom that has been hidden and that God destined for our glory before time began. ⁸None of the rulers of this age understood it, for if they had, they would not have crucified the Lord of glory. ⁹However, as it is written: "**What no eye has seen, what no ear has heard, and what no human mind has conceived**"— the things God has prepared for those who love him— ¹⁰these are the things God has **revealed** to us by his **Spirit**. The **Spirit** searches all things, **even the deep things of God**. ¹¹For who among men knows the thoughts of a man except the man's spirit within him? **In the same way no one knows the thoughts of God except the Spirit of God.** ¹²What we have received is not the spirit of the world, but the **Spirit** who is from God, **so** that we may **understand** what God has freely given us. ¹³This is what we speak, not in words taught us by human wisdom but **in words taught by the Spirit**, explaining spiritual realities with Spirit-taught words. ¹⁴**The person without the Spirit does not accept the things that come from the Spirit of God** but considers them foolishness, and cannot understand them because **they are discerned only through the Spirit.**

1 Corinthians 2: 6-14

I have endeavoured to share the deep truths of the Word of God with you in this Chapter as much as the **Holy Spirit** has **revealed** them to me. **Hence, it is essential for believers not to preoccupy themselves with the perishable things of this world by chasing only after financial and material prosperity and the things that rot, but rather to seek the deep things of God that not only brings abundant life through our Lord Jesus Christ, but also enables us to enjoy Kingdom living on earth, whilst preparing for eternity as well.**

*²³Yet a time is coming and has now come when the **true worshipers** will worship the Father in the **Spirit** and in truth, for they are the kind of worshipers the Father seeks. ²⁴**God is spirit**, and his worshipers **must worship** in the **Spirit** and in truth."*

<u>*John 4: 23-24*</u>

¹⁰The thief comes only to steal and kill and destroy; I have come that they may have life, and have it to the full.

<u>*John 10: 10*</u>

It is my prayer that as you prayerfully read the words and Bible passages in this chapter **over and over again,** to specifically and fervently ask the **Holy Spirit** to come into your life and dwell in you, **to filter, to fill,** and **to empower you,** and after your fervent prayers, that you will indeed be filtered of every impurity that is not of God and that He will fill you with His indwelling presence and then empower you to live the victorious Christian life in the mighty name of Jesus Christ, amen.

CHAPTER 5

The Holy Spirit

This chapter on the Holy Spirit has seven sub-headings depicting the person of the Holy Spirit. The sub-headings are listed below, whilst the next chapter, titled *Living a life that is filled with the Holy Spirit*, explains more on what we will experience when we allow the Holy Spirit to have a permanent residence in our lives.

The Promise of the Holy Spirit

The Arrival of the Holy Spirit

The Works of the Holy Spirit

The Wisdom of the Holy Spirit

The Fruit of the Holy Spirit

The Power of the Holy Spirit

Life through the Holy Spirit

The Promise of the Holy Spirit

[26]I will give you a new heart and put a new spirit in you; I will remove from you your heart of stone and give you a heart of flesh. [27]And I will put my Spirit in you and move you to follow my decrees and be careful to keep my laws.

Ezekiel 36: 26-27

[15]"If you love me, keep my commands. [16]And I will ask the Father, and he will give you another advocate to help you and be with you forever— [17]the Spirit of truth. The world cannot accept him, because it neither sees him nor knows him. But you know him, for he lives with you and will be in you."

John 14: 15-17

4On one occasion, while he was eating with them, he gave them this command: "Do not leave Jerusalem, but wait for the gift my Father promised, which you have heard me speak about. 5For John baptized with water, but in a few days you will be baptized with the Holy Spirit."

Acts 1: 4-5

The Arrival of the Holy Spirit

1When the day of Pentecost came, they were all together in one place. 2Suddenly a sound like the blowing of a violent wind came from heaven and filled the whole house where they were sitting. 3They saw what seemed to be tongues of fire that separated and came to rest on each of them. 4All of them were filled with the Holy Spirit and began to speak in other tongues (or other languages) as the Spirit enabled them.

Acts 2: 1-4

The Works of the Holy Spirit

Teacher

26But the Advocate, the Holy Spirit, whom the Father will send in my name, will teach you all things and will remind you of everything I have said to you.

John 14: 26

Revealer

26"When the Advocate comes, whom I will send to you from the Father—the Spirit of truth who goes out from the Father—he will testify about me."

John 15: 26

Guide

12"I have much more to say to you, more than you can now bear. 13But when he, the Spirit of truth, comes, he will guide you into all the truth. He will not speak on his own; he will speak only what he hears, and he will tell you what is yet to come."

John 16: 12-13

Intercessor

*²⁶In the same way, the Spirit helps us in our weakness. We do not know what we ought to pray for, but the Spirit himself **intercedes** for us through **wordless groans**. ²⁷And he who searches our hearts knows the mind of the Spirit, because the **Spirit intercedes for God's people** in accordance with the **will** of God.*

Romans 8: 26-27

Companion

²⁰Here I am! I stand at the door and knock. If anyone hears my voice and opens the door, I will come in and eat with that person, and they with me.

Revelation 3: 20

The Wisdom of the Holy Spirit

*¹And so it was with me, brothers and sisters. When I came to you, I did not come with eloquence or human wisdom as I proclaimed to you the testimony about God. ²For I resolved to know nothing while I was with you except Jesus Christ and him crucified. ³I came to you in weakness with great fear and trembling. ⁴**My message and my preaching were not with wise and persuasive words, but with a demonstration of the Spirit's power, ⁵so that your faith might not rest on human wisdom, but on God's power.***

1 Corinthians 2: 1-5

The Fruit of the Holy Spirit

*²²But the **fruit of the Spirit** is love, joy, peace, forbearance, kindness, goodness, faithfulness, ²³gentleness and self-control. Against such things there is no law. ²⁴Those who belong to Christ Jesus have crucified the flesh with its passions and desires. ²⁵Since we live by the Spirit, let us keep in step with the Spirit. ²⁶Let us not become conceited, provoking and envying each other.*

Galatians 5: 22-26

The Power of the Holy Spirit

[14]*For this reason I kneel before the Father,* [15]*from whom every family in heaven and on earth derives its name.* [16]*I pray that out of his glorious riches he may strengthen you with* **power through his Spirit in your inner being,** [17]*so that Christ may dwell in your hearts through faith. And I pray that you, being rooted and established in love,* [18]*may have* **power,** *together with all the Lord's holy people, to grasp how wide and long and high and deep is the love of Christ,* [19]*and to know this love that surpasses knowledge—that you may be filled to the measure of all the fullness of God.* [20]*Now to him who is able to do immeasurably more than all we ask or imagine, according to his power that is at work within us,* [21]*to him be glory in the church and in Christ Jesus throughout all generations, for ever and ever! Amen.*

Ephesians 3: 14-21

Life through the Holy Spirit

[5]*Those who live according to the flesh have their minds set on what the flesh desires; but those who live in accordance with the Spirit have their minds set on what the Spirit desires.* [6]*The mind governed by the flesh is death, but the mind governed by the Spirit is life and peace.* [7]*The mind governed by the flesh is hostile to God; it does not submit to God's law, nor can it do so.* [8]*Those who are in the realm of the flesh cannot please God.* [9]*You, however, are not in the realm of the flesh but are in the realm of the Spirit, if indeed the Spirit of God lives in you. And if anyone does not have the Spirit of Christ, they do not belong to Christ.* [10]*But if Christ is in you, then even though your body is subject to death because of sin, the Spirit gives life because of righteousness.* [11]*And if the Spirit of him who raised Jesus from the dead is living in you, he who raised Christ from the dead will also give life to your mortal bodies because of his Spirit who lives in you.* [12]*Therefore, brothers and sisters, we have an obligation—but it is not to the flesh, to live according to it.* [13]*For if you live according to the flesh, you will die; but if by the Spirit you put to death the misdeeds of the body, you will live.* [14]*For those who are led by the Spirit of God are the children of God.* [15]*The Spirit you received does not make you slaves, so that you live in fear again; rather, the Spirit you received brought about your adoption to sonship. And by him we cry, "Abba, Father."*

[16]*The Spirit himself testifies with our spirit that we are God's children.* [17]*Now if we are children, then we are heirs—heirs of God and co-heirs with Christ, if indeed we share in his sufferings in order that we may also share in his glory.*

Romans 8: 5-17

CHAPTER 6

Living a life that is filled with the Holy Spirit

The question is sometimes asked: 'How do you know when you are living a life that is filled with the Holy Spirit?'

Yes, the teaching in *Galatians 5: 22-23* gives us a good insight on how you may know that you are living a life that is filled with the Holy Spirit. However, in order to better understand the significance of what is written in verses 22-23 which we elaborated upon in the previous chapter, let us go back a bit and look again at what the scriptures say in *Galatians 5: 16-21*.

[16]So I say, live by the Spirit, and you will not gratify the desires of the sinful nature (flesh). [17]For the sinful nature (flesh) desires what is contrary to the Spirit, and the Spirit what is contrary to the sinful nature (flesh). They are in conflict with each other, so that you do not do what you want. [19]The acts of the sinful nature are obvious: sexual immorality, impurity and debauchery (i.e. extreme indulgence in bodily pleasures and especially sexual pleasures); [20]idolatry and witchcraft; hatred, discord, jealousy, fits of rage, selfish ambition, dissensions (i.e. disagreement that causes the people in a group to argue about something that is important to them), factions; [21]and envy (i.e. a feeling of discontented or resentful longing aroused by someone else's possessions, qualities, or luck); drunkenness, orgies, and the like. I warn you, as I did before, that those who live like this will not inherit the kingdom of God.'

Galatians 5: 16-21

Now, compare verses **16-21** with verses **22-23**, which reads as follows: ²²But the fruit of the Spirit is love, joy, peace, patience, kindness, goodness, faithfulness, ²³gentleness and self-control. Against such things there is no law.'

To put it simply, when you are living a life that is filled with the Holy Spirit, it will be obvious, because you will manifest the fruit of the Holy Spirit in every area of your life. For example, if your life is full of love, you will know, because you will simply radiate love, both internally and externally.

Also, if there is no joy in your life, that is an indication that something is not right and you will need to ask yourself, why and what is stealing your joy. Moreover, if you lack peace and you are constantly troubled, that may be an indication that you are yet to surrender your life fully to our Lord Jesus Christ, because He taught us not to worry (**Matthew 6: 25-34, Philippians 4: 6-7, 1 Peter 5:7**).

There may however be occasions or instances when we may have reasons to be sad (e.g. periods of bereavement etc.), but then, it must be only for a period, because the scripture says:

²⁸And we know that in all things God works for the good of those who love Him, who have been called according to His purpose

<u>Romans 8:28</u>

To find your bearing with respect to whether or not you are living a life that is filled with the Holy Spirit, you may wish to examine yourself against the other fruits of the Holy Spirit. For example: Are you patient? Are you a kind person? Are you filled with goodness? Are you faithful? Are you gentle? More importantly, are you in control of your temperament at all times? Someone reading this book might think that I am being impractical by expecting people to live by these expectations. What you need to remember is the fact that I did not write any of the Bible passages we looked at in the previous chapter on Holy Spirit.

Besides, if we allow ourselves to be filled with the Holy Spirit, we will be the beneficiaries, because not only will we live a victorious Christian life and be good witnesses for our Lord Jesus Christ, but we will also be assured of our place in heaven when we depart this world. It really is a win–win situation.

Sinful Nature (The flesh)

The sinful nature is better described in **Romans 7: 14-25**, where we see how our flesh is constantly at war with the Holy Spirit. For example, Paul wrote that what I want to do, I do not do, but what I hate to do, I do.

Our sinful nature (flesh) wants to do its own thing which is different from what the Holy Spirit wants us to do. This explains why we must fully understand the workings of the Holy Spirit and the workings of the flesh. **The question then for us is: Which is the dominant influence in our lives? Is it the Holy Spirit or is it our flesh?** Do we allow the desires of our flesh to rule and control our lives or do we allow the Holy Spirit to control and rule the way we live our lives?

Five Keys to Living a Holy Spirit-Filled Life

1. Renew your mind

The first key to living a life that is filled with the Holy Spirit is the need to renew our minds. In the *Book of Romans*, Apostle Paul wrote as follows:

[1]'Therefore, I urge you, brothers, in view of God's mercy, to offer your bodies as living sacrifices, holy and pleasing to God—this is your spiritual act of

worship. ²*Do not conform any longer to the pattern of this world, but be transformed by the renewing of your mind ...'*

Romans 12: 1-2

2. Repent from sins

The second key is the need to repent from our sins

¹*'What shall we say, then? Shall we go on sinning, so that grace may increase? ²By no means! We died to sin; how can we live in it any longer?'*

Romans 6: 1-2

3. Seek God with all your heart

The third key to living life through the Holy Spirit is to seek God with all your heart.

¹³*'You will seek me and find me when you seek me with all your heart.'*

Jeremiah 29: 13

4. Have complete faith in God

The fourth key is to have complete faith in God through our Lord Jesus Christ and yield (submit) to the Holy Spirit.

²²*"Have faith in God," Jesus answered. ²³"Truly I tell you, if anyone says to this mountain, 'Go, throw yourself into the sea,' and does not doubt in their heart but believes that what they say will happen, it will be done for them.*

Mark 11: 22-23

⁶*"And without faith it is impossible to please God, anyone who comes to him must believe that he exists and that he rewards those who earnestly seek him."*

Hebrews 11: 6

5. Feed the Holy Spirit

The fifth key is to feed the Holy Spirit

*[2]After fasting for forty days and forty nights, he was hungry. [3]The tempter came and said to Him, "If you are the Son of God, tell these stones to become bread." [4]Jesus answered, "It is written: 'Man does not live on bread alone, but on **every word** that comes from the mouth of God'".*

Matthew 4: 2-4

The reason many Christians experience defeat is because they are not filled with the Holy Spirit. One of the key blessings of the Holy Spirit is that his indwelling presence in our lives provides us with the **power** to resist the devil and thus live a life that glorifies our LORD God almighty 24/7.

Therefore, in order to enjoy a life that is truly filled with the Holy Spirit, you must be alert at all times. Study the Word of God (Holy Bible) and stay sensitive to His Spirit. Feed your spirit daily by reading all kinds of daily devotionals.

Finally, allow the Holy Spirit to be the dominant influence in your life at all times through his **power** that dwells in you. That way, you will be empowered to refuse and reject the evil desires of your flesh whenever it flares up and seeks attention.

CHAPTER 7

Prayer

What Is Prayer?

Prayer is an invocation or an act that seeks to activate a rapport with an object of worship through deliberate communication. In the narrow sense, the term refers to an act of supplication or intercession directed towards God.

Prayer can also be described as an act that we engage with in order to enforce the willingness of our LORD God almighty through our supplications to perform what He has already promised us in His Words, as against compelling His reluctance to bless us. Our Father in Heaven is always willing to bless us as demonstrated by our Lord Jesus Christ in the first chapter of Book of Mark.

40A man with leprosy came to him and begged him on his knees, "If you are willing, you can make me clean." 41Filled with compassion, Jesus reached out his hand and touched the man. "I am willing," he said. "Be clean!" 42Immediately the leprosy left him and he was cured.

Mark 1:40-42

How Should We Pray?

Kneeling down, standing up, jumping up and down, silently, loudly, shouting, singing, prostrating, on a hard floor, on a mat, by our bedside, inside the house, outside the house, inside the church, on top of a mountain, etc.

Our Lord Jesus Christ on Prayer

⁵"And when you pray, **do not be like the hypocrites**, for they love to pray standing in the synagogues and on the street corners **to be seen by others**. Truly I tell you, they have received their reward in full. ⁶But when you pray, go into your room, close the door and pray to your Father, who is unseen. Then your Father, who sees what is done in secret, will reward you. ⁷**And when you pray, do not keep on babbling like pagans, for they think they will be heard because of their many words.** ⁸Do not be like them, for your Father knows what you need before you ask him.

Matthew 6: 5-8

⁹"This, then, is how you should pray: 'Our Father in heaven, hallowed be your name, ¹⁰your kingdom come, **your will be done**, on earth as it is in heaven. ¹¹Give us today our daily bread. ¹²And **forgive us** our debts, as we also have forgiven our debtors. ¹³And lead us not into temptation, but deliver us from the evil one.' ¹⁴For if you **forgive** other people when they sin against you, your heavenly Father will also forgive you. ¹⁵**But if you do not forgive others their sins, your Father will not forgive your sins."**

Matthew 6: 9-15

²²**"Have faith in God,"** Jesus answered.

²³"Truly I tell you, if anyone says to this mountain, 'Go, throw yourself into the sea,' and **does not doubt** in their heart but **believes** that what they say will happen, it will be done for them.

Mark 11: 22-23

Paul on Prayer

⁶Do **not be anxious** about anything, but in every situation, by prayer and petition, **with thanksgiving**, present your requests to God. ⁷And the **peace of God**, which transcends all understanding, will guard your hearts and your minds in Christ Jesus.

Philippians 4: 6-7

When Should We Pray?

17Pray without ceasing.

1 Thessalonians 5:17

*Then Jesus told his disciples a parable to show them that **they should always pray and not give up**. 2He said: "In a certain town there was a judge who neither feared God nor cared what people thought. 3And there was a widow in that town who kept coming to him with the plea, 'Grant me justice against my adversary.' 4For some time he refused. But finally he said to himself, 'Even though I don't fear God or care what people think, 5yet because this widow keeps bothering me, I will see that she gets justice, so that she won't eventually wear me out with her coming!'"*

Luke 18:1-5

What Do You Ask for When You Pray?

Do you ask for blessings or do you rain curses on your enemies?

6Blessed are those who hunger and thirst for righteousness, for they will be filled.

Matthew 5: 6

43"You have heard that it was said, 'Love your neighbour and hate your enemy.' 44But I tell you, love your enemies and pray for those who persecute you, 45that you may be sons of your Father in heaven. HE causes HIS sun to rise on the evil and the good, and sends rain on the righteous and the unrighteous.

Matthew 5: 43-44

How Do You Live Your Life—for Christ or for Yourself?

Is your lifestyle holy and righteous or are you living in sin?

*15But just as he who called you is holy, so **be holy** in all you do; 16for it is written: **"Be holy, because I am holy."***

1 Peter 1 :15-16

Are Your Prayers in Line with the Word and Will of God?

Are your prayers flesh-driven or inspired by the Holy Spirit?

³When you ask, you do not receive, because you ask with wrong motives, that you may spend what you get on your pleasures.

James 4: 3

Prayer of a Righteous Person

*¹⁶Therefore **confess** your sins to each other and pray for each other so that you may be healed. The **prayer** of a **righteous person** is **powerful and effective**.*

James 5: 16

Do You Abide?

*⁵"I am the vine, you are the branches. He who **abides in Me**, and I in him, bears much fruit; for without Me you can do nothing. ⁶ If anyone **does not abide in Me**, he is cast out as a branch and is withered; and they gather them and throw them into the fire, and they are burned. ⁷ If you **abide in Me**, and My words **abide in** you, you will ask whatever you desire, and it shall be done for you. ⁸ By this My Father is glorified, that you bear much fruit; so you will be My disciples."*

John 15: 5-8

Who is the Person Praying?

Does **our LORD God almighty know you**? Do you have a personal relationship with HIM?

*¹⁶As soon as Jesus was baptised, he went up out of the water. At that moment heaven was opened, and he saw the Spirit of God descending like a dove and alighting on him. ¹⁷ And a voice from heaven said, "**This is my Son**, whom I love; with him I am well pleased."*

Matthew 3: 16-17

31"When the Son of Man comes in his glory, and all the angels with him, he will sit on his glorious throne. 32 All the nations will be gathered before him, and he will separate the people one from another as a shepherd separates the sheep from the goats. 33 He will put the sheep on his right and the goats on his left. 34 Then the King will say to those on his right, 'Come, you who are blessed by my Father; take your inheritance, the kingdom prepared for you since the creation of the world. 35 For I was hungry and you gave me something to eat, I was thirsty and you gave me something to drink, I was a stranger and you invited me in, 36I needed clothes and you clothed me, I was sick and you looked after me, I was in prison and you came to visit me.'

Matthew 25: 31-36

11God did extraordinary miracles through Paul, 12so that even handkerchiefs and aprons that had touched him were taken to the sick, and their illnesses were cured and the evil spirits left them. 13Some Jews who went around driving out evil spirits tried to invoke the name of the Lord Jesus over those who were demon-possessed. They would say, "In the name of the Jesus whom Paul preaches, I command you to come out." 14Seven sons of Sceva, a Jewish chief priest, were doing this. 15One day the evil spirit answered them, "Jesus I know, and Paul I know about, but who are you?" 16Then the man who had the evil spirit jumped on them and overpowered them all. He gave them such a beating that they ran out of the house naked and bleeding.

Acts 19: 11-16

The key point here is that **our LORD God almighty answers the person praying** and not necessarily the prayer, which explains why the prayer of a righteous person is described in *James 5: 16* as powerful and effective.

Hindrances to Prayers

Daniel's experience

11And he said to me, "O Daniel, man greatly beloved, understand the words that I speak to you, and stand upright, for I have now been sent to you." While he was speaking this word to me, I stood trembling. 12Then he said to me, "Do not fear, Daniel, for from the first day that you set your heart to understand, and to humble yourself before your God, your words were heard; and I have come because of your words. [13]**But the prince of the kingdom of Persia withstood me twenty-one days; and behold, Michael, one of the chief princes, came to help me, for I had been left alone there with the kings of Persia.** [14]Now I have come to make you understand what will happen to your people in the latter days, for the vision refers to many days yet to come."

Daniel 10: 11-14

Prayer of Agreement

[18]*"Truly I tell you, whatever you bind on earth will be bound in heaven, and whatever you loose on earth will be loosed in heaven.* [19]*Again, truly I tell you that **if two of you on earth agree about anything they ask for**, it will be done for them by my Father in heaven."*

Matthew 18: 18-19

Pray with Confidence

[16]*Let us then approach the throne of grace with **confidence**, so that we may receive mercy and find grace to help us in our time of need.*

Hebrews 4: 16

[14]*This is the **confidence** we have in approaching God: that if we ask anything according to **HIS will**, HE hears us.* [15]*And if we know that HE hears us—whatever we ask—we know that we have what we asked of HIM.*

1 John 5: 14-15

CHAPTER 8

Prayers and Answers:
Is Faith alone enough?

The Faith of the Centurion

*⁵When Jesus had entered Capernaum, a centurion came to him, asking for help. ⁶"Lord," he said, "my servant lies at home paralyzed, suffering terribly." ⁷Jesus said to him, "Shall I come and heal him?" ⁸The centurion replied, "Lord, I do not deserve to have you come under my roof. But just say the word, and my servant will be healed. ⁹For I myself am a man under authority, with soldiers under me. I tell this one, 'Go,' and he goes; and that one, 'Come,' and he comes. I say to my servant, 'Do this,' and he does it." ¹⁰When Jesus heard this, he was amazed and said to those following him, "Truly I tell you, I have not found anyone in Israel with such **great faith**. ¹¹I say to you that many will come from the east and the west, and will take their places at the feast with Abraham, Isaac and Jacob in the kingdom of heaven. ¹²But the subjects of the kingdom will be thrown outside, into the darkness, where there will be weeping and gnashing of teeth." ¹³Then Jesus said to the centurion, "Go! Let it be done just as you believed it would." And his servant was healed at that moment.*

Matthew 8: 5-13

As you can see from the above passage, Our Lord Jesus Christ commended the Centurion as having **great faith**. Hence, the question in this chapter: **Is faith alone enough in order for our prayers to be answered**?

The generally held view is that **Faith** on its own may not be enough in certain circumstances, as it has to be anchored with the following additional kingdom ingredients:

1. **Obedience**
2. **Forgiveness**
3. **Holiness**
4. **Thanksgiving**

The ingredients—**faith, obedience, forgiveness, holiness** and the spirit of **thanksgiving**—work together in order for us to experience open heavens and unrestricted answers to prayers, just like our Lord Jesus Christ experienced when he walked on earth.

Our LORD God almighty starts His work when we stop fretting and worrying, hence it is imperative that we learn to '**Let go and Let God', otherwise our prayers are just empty words**. Yes, I repeat, our LORD God almighty starts His work on our prayers when we **stop worrying** and we **start trusting** Him.

It starts with **obedience** to the teachings of our Lord Jesus Christ, followed by a heart that is slow to anger and **forgives** very quickly. Living in **holiness** and **righteousness** is critical, whilst having a heart that is **thankful** is non-negotiable.

The key question is: **Can you do all of the above through your own strength**? The simple answer is categorical **No**. It is absolutely impossible to accomplish through the workings of the flesh. The indwelling presence of the Holy Spirit in you as a person is the answer because the **Holy Spirit** is our **Advocate, Counsellor, Comforter, Encourager, Enabler** and constant **Companion**. His indwelling presence in our lives **is tantamount to having our God almighty living inside us**.

The implication is that if our God almighty lives inside us, how then will He not hear us or answer us when we cry to Him? After all, our Lord Jesus Christ told us categorically in **Matthew 7: 7** to ask, seek and knock. He also told us in **Mark 11: 22-23** to believe that we have received when we ask. Are there conditions to these categorical statements? Of course, yes, there are.

They are re-emphasised below.

Faith

Faith is the **spiritual oil** that fires our prayer engines.

¹Now *faith is the substance of things hoped for, the evidence of things not seen.*

Hebrews 11: 1

⁶*And **without faith** it is impossible to please God, because anyone who comes to him must believe that he exists and that he rewards those who earnestly seek him.*

Hebrews 11: 6

³⁵*That day when evening came, He said to His disciples, 'Let us go over to the other side'. ³⁶Leaving the crowd behind, they took Him along, just as He was, in the boat. There were also other boats with Him. ³⁷A furious squall came up, and the waves broke over the boat, so that it was nearly swamped. ³⁸Jesus was in the stern, sleeping on a cushion. The disciples woke Him and said to Him, 'Teacher, don't you care if we drown?' ³⁹He got up, rebuked the wind and said to the waves, 'Quiet! Be still!' Then the wind died down and it was completely calm. ⁴⁰He said to His disciples, '**Why are you so afraid? Do you still have no faith?**'*

Mark 4: 35-40

Obedience

Obedience is like **a sweet aroma** that pleases our God almighty.

*²²But Samuel replied: "Does the LORD delight in burnt offerings and sacrifices as much as in obeying the LORD? To **obey** is better than sacrifice, and to heed is better than the fat of rams. ²³For rebellion is like the sin of divination, and arrogance like the evil of idolatry. Because you have rejected the word of the LORD, he has rejected you as king."*

1 Samuel 15: 22-23

*²⁵"Therefore I tell you, **do not worry** about your life, what you will eat or drink; or about your body, what you will wear. Is not life more important than food, and the body more important than clothes? ²⁶Look at the birds of the air; they do not sow or reap or store away in barns, and yet your heavenly Father feeds them. Are you not much more valuable than they? ²⁷Who of you by **worrying** can add a single hour to your life? ²⁸"And why do you **worry** about clothes? See how the flowers of the field grow. They do not labour or spin. ²⁹Yet I tell you that not even Solomon in all his splendour was dressed like one of these. ³⁰If that is how God clothes the grass of the field, which is here today and tomorrow is thrown into the fire, will he not much more clothe you, O you of little faith? ³¹So **do not worry**, saying, 'What shall we eat?' or 'What shall we drink?' or 'What shall we wear?' ³²For the pagans run after all these things, and your heavenly Father knows that you need them. ³³But seek first his kingdom and his righteousness, and all these things will be given to you as well. ³⁴Therefore **do not worry** about tomorrow, for tomorrow will **worry** about itself. Each day has enough trouble of its own.*

Matthew 6:25-34

The implication of the above passages is that in order to enjoy an effective and efficacious prayer life, it is **imperative that you stop worrying and start trusting** our LORD God almighty and His promises, **because saying you have faith and worrying at the same time is actually a demonstration of lack of faith and indeed an act of disobedience.**

Forgiveness

Forgiveness takes us to **the realms of divinity**; for to err is human, but to forgive is divine.

*¹²And **forgive us** our debts, as we also have forgiven our debtors. ¹⁴For if you **forgive** other people when they sin against you, your heavenly Father will also forgive you. ¹⁵But if you do not **forgive** others their sins, your Father will not **forgive** your sins.*

Matthew 6: 12, 14-15

Holiness

Holiness is **our bodily offering** that allows our LORD God almighty to **dwell in us**.

*¹Therefore, I urge you, brothers, in view of God's mercy, **to offer your bodies as living sacrifices, holy and pleasing to God**—this is your spiritual act of worship.*

Romans 12: 1

*¹⁴Make every effort to live in peace with everyone and to be **holy**; without **holiness** no one will see the Lord. Strive for peace with everyone, and for **holiness** without which no one will see the Lord.*

Hebrews 12: 14

Thanksgiving

Thanksgiving **kindles our spirit** and **reminds us of our humanity,** in that we can do nothing by our own power and that answers to all our prayers come when we ask in the mighty name of our Lord Jesus Christ.

*⁶Do not be anxious about anything, but in every situation, by prayer and petition, **with thanksgiving**, present your requests to God.*

Philippians 4: 6

¹⁸*Do not get drunk on wine, which leads to debauchery. Instead, be filled with the Spirit,* ¹⁹*speaking to one another with psalms, hymns, and songs from the Spirit. Sing and make music from your heart to the LORD,* ²⁰**always giving thanks to God the Father for everything**, *in the name of our Lord Jesus Christ.*

Ephesians 5: 18-20

¹¹ *Now on his way to Jerusalem, Jesus travelled along the border between Samaria and Galilee.* ¹² *As he was going into a village, ten men who had leprosy met him. They stood at a distance* ¹³ *and called out in a loud voice, "Jesus, Master, have pity on us!"* ¹⁴ *When he saw them, he said, "Go, show yourselves to the priests." And as they went, they were cleansed.* ¹⁵ **One of them, when he saw he was healed, came back, praising God in a loud voice.** ¹⁶ **He threw himself at Jesus' feet and thanked him**—*and he was a Samaritan.* ¹⁷ *Jesus asked, "Were not all ten cleansed? Where are the other nine?* ¹⁸ **Has no one returned to give praise to God except this foreigner?"** ¹⁹ *Then he said to him, "Rise and go; your faith has made you well."*

Luke 17:11-19

God

Perhaps without any shadow or scintilla of doubt, the most important element is the role of our **LORD God almighty** in answering our prayers, **our glorious Father in Heaven who makes the impossible possible and reverses the irreversible**. Yes, He is the one entity that answers our prayers when we ask in the name of His precious Son, our Lord Jesus Christ.

²³*In that day you will no longer ask me anything. Very truly I tell you,* **my Father** *will give you* **whatever you ask in my name.** ²⁴*Until now you have not asked for anything in my name. Ask and you will receive, and your joy will be complete.*

John 16: 23-24

⁵*What, after all, is Apollos? And what is Paul? Only servant, through whom you came to believe-as the Lord has assigned to each his task.* ⁶*I planted the*

seed, Apollos watered it, but God has been making it grow. [7]So neither the one who plants nor the who waters is anything, **but only God, who makes things grow**.

<u>1Corinthians 3:7</u>

CHAPTER 9

Living Sacrifices

Romans 12 is one of the most pivotal chapters in the Bible with regard to our Christian walk. From the first verse to the last, the teachings in *Romans 12* challenges us by its demands in almost every verse to do the very opposite of what our flesh would ordinarily want us to do. Hence, these teachings should be used as a barometer for reflection and reset in our Christian walk. Let us now look at each verse and see what it offers us.

Romans 12

¹Therefore, I urge you, brothers and sisters, in view of God's mercy, to offer your bodies as living sacrifices, holy and pleasing to God—this is your spiritual act of worship.

²Do not conform any longer to the pattern of this world, but be transformed by the renewing of your mind. Then you will be able to test and approve what God's will is—his good, pleasing and perfect will.

³For by the grace given me I say to every one of you: Do not think of yourself more highly than you ought, but rather think of yourself with sober judgment, in accordance with the measure of faith God has given you.

⁴Just as each of us has one body with many members, and these members do not all have the same function,

⁵so in Christ we who are many, form one body, and each member belongs to all the others.

⁶*We have different gifts, according to the grace given to each of us. If a man's gift is prophesying, let him use it in proportion to his faith.*

⁷*If it is serving, let him serve; if it is teaching, let him teach;*

⁸*if it is to encourage, let him encourage; if it is contributing to the needs of others, let him give generously; if it is leadership, let him govern diligently; if it is to showing mercy, let him do it cheerfully.*

Love in Action

⁹*Love must be sincere. Hate what is evil; cling to what is good.*

¹⁰*Be devoted to one another in brotherly love. Honour one another above yourselves.*

¹¹*Never be lacking in zeal, but keep your spiritual fervour, serving the Lord.*

¹²*Be joyful in hope, patient in affliction, faithful in prayer.*

¹³*Share with God's people who are in need. Practice hospitality.*

¹⁴*Bless those who persecute you; bless and do not curse.*

¹⁵*Rejoice with those who rejoice; mourn with those who mourn.*

¹⁶*Live in harmony with one another. Do not be proud, but be willing to associate with people of low position. Do not be conceited.*

¹⁷*Do not repay anyone evil for evil. Be careful to do what is right in the eyes of everybody.*

¹⁸*If it is possible, as far as it depends on you, live at peace with everyone.*

¹⁹*Do not take revenge, my dear friends, but leave room for God's wrath, for it is written: "It is mine to avenge; I will repay," says the Lord.*

²⁰*On the contrary: "If your enemy is hungry, feed him; if he is thirsty, give him something to drink. In doing this, you will heap burning coals on his head."*

²¹*Do not be overcome by evil, but overcome evil with good.*

Why Is Romans 12 as Important as Romans 8?

In this chapter, we will focus on Romans 12 and touch on Romans 8 at the end because of its emphasis on holy living and the empowerment to do so through our **submission** to the Holy Spirit. In order to have a fuller understanding of *Romans 12*, I suggest that believers spend some time to prayerfully read the whole of *Romans 5, 6, 7, 8* and *10*.

The teachings in these chapters when read together can be life changing in our Christian walk, particularly for those who desire to have a deeper relationship with our Lord Jesus Christ through the help of the Holy Spirit. The result is an empowerment to experience the '**Kingdom of Heaven Here and Now**' whilst still here on planet earth.

The question that arises is, how can believers offer their bodies as living sacrifices, holy and pleasing to God, as required in *verse 1*? The reality of offering our bodies as living sacrifices implies that you give something up, particularly something that gives you pleasure in one form or another. For instance, sexual pleasure with multiple partners outside of marriage. Indulging in drunkenness or drug abuse is another. That is why *verse 2* states categorically that we should no longer conform to the pattern of this world where everything goes. Our young people are most at risk because they are impressionable and vulnerable to what they see on TV or read on social media. It is easy for them to get carried away and think that the types of behaviour exhibited by actors, musicians, and social influencers who engage in multiple divorces and ungodly acts including same-gender relationships, sex changes, and drug abuse are okay. Sadly, they are not okay for believers and it is our responsibility to say so to our children and guide them on the path of holiness and righteousness. *Matthew 16: 24-25* is also instructive on the point.

Verse 3 admonishes us to expunge acts of pride and spiritual arrogance from our lives. It is important to appreciate that all our abilities and know-how are gifts from our LORD God almighty. We are all given a measure of faith and how we exercise it determines the nature of the relationship we have and enjoy with our Father in Heaven through our Lord Jesus Christ.

Verses 4, 5, 6, 7 and **8** expound on the need for the Church (Ekklesia) i.e. the body of Christ to work together by using all the gifts and abilities giving to different members of the church. For example, if a man's gift is to lead the church, let him do so diligently with sincerity and let the members of the church support him. If a woman has the ability to sing, please let her sing in a manner that brings glory to our LORD God almighty.

In essence, there should not be any kind of jealousy or envying of each other's gifts or abilities within the body of Christ when they are exhibited. Rather, the whole church should work together selflessly to glorify our LORD God almighty and His precious Son, our Lord and Saviour Jesus Christ.

Verses 9 and **10** focus on sincere love and brotherly love whilst hating what is evil and clinging to what is good. The demand to honour others above ourselves is worthy of special attention. This is very important and a good reason to expunge pride and the sense of self-importance over others from our individual psyche.

Verse 11 touches on aspects of our lives that are often overlooked. That is, the word "zeal" which is described as great energy or enthusiasm in the pursuit of a cause or an objective. Thus, Paul asks us not to lack zeal as we keep our spiritual fervour whilst serving our LORD God almighty at the same time.

I am particularly touched by the encouragement given to us in **verse 12, 'to be joyful in hope, patient in affliction, faithful in prayer'**. This verse speaks volumes for most Christians today in various parts of the world as they face all kinds of challenges and tribulations. **Ephesian 6: 12** tells us that **'our struggle is not against**

flesh and blood, but against the rulers, against the authorities, against the powers of this dark world and against the spiritual forces of evil in the heavenly realms'.

With this realisation in mind, it says a lot for believers to be joyful as they hope and wait for answers to their prayers; patient during the period of affliction because the period of affliction shall also surely pass; and more importantly to remain faithful in their prayer life because the answers will definitely come **'for those who hope in the LORD shall renew their strength; they will soar on wings like eagles; they will run and not grow weary, they will walk and not be faint'** (*Isaiah 40: 31*).

The teachings in *verses 13* to *20* are self-explanatory, but I must confess that I find *verse 21* to be highly and particularly instructive in that **we are told not to be overcome by evil, but to overcome evil will with good**. The story of Joseph and his brothers is a good example of how to overcome evil with good. Most of us are familiar with the story of how his brothers sold him into slavery and told their father that he was killed by a wild animal. He was subsequently bought by Potiphar, one of Pharaoh's officials.

At some point, Potiphar's wife became attracted to him, but he refused her advances and fled from her with his clothes in her hand. With her lies against Joseph, Potiphar put Joseph in the King's prison. Whilst in prison, Joseph helped Pharaoh to interpret his dreams. The rest as they say is history as he became the Prime Minister of Egypt when Pharaoh put him in charge of the whole of Egypt. Joseph's interpretation of Pharaoh's dreams helped Egypt and the surrounding nations during the seven years of famine.

When Joseph's father died, his brothers became afraid thinking that he still had a grudge against them and would now punish them for what they did to him. His reaction to his brothers' entreaties to him in *Genesis 50: 19-21* best describes what it means **'not to be overcome by evil, but to overcome evil with good'.**

*¹⁹But Joseph said to them, "Don't be afraid. Am I in the place of God? ²⁰**You intended to harm me, but God intended it for good to accomplish what is now being done, the saving of many lives.** ²¹So then, don't be afraid. I will provide for you and your children." And he reassured them and spoke kindly to them.*

Genesis 50: 19-21

Having looked deeply at *Romans 12*, the key question is how can we live our lives in a manner that is holy and pleasing to God? Can we do it with our will power or human strength? Absolutely not, and that is why it is worth looking at what Paul wrote:

⁵'Those who live according to the flesh have their minds set on what the flesh desires; but those who live in accordance with the Spirit have their minds set on what the Spirit desires'.

Romans 8: 5

In simple terms, what enables a believer in our Lord Jesus Christ to offer his/her body as a living sacrifice, holy and pleasing to God, and as a spiritual act of worship is the Holy Spirit. **When a believer submits to God, abides in our Lord Jesus Christ and is led by the Holy Spirit,** he/she will be empowered to live and enjoy the **'Kingdom of Heaven Here and Now'** experience that also assures us of eternity with our LORD God almighty when our time on earth comes to an end in the mighty name of Jesus Christ, amen.

CHAPTER 10

Do You Love God?

*⁵**Love the Lord your God** with all your heart and with all your soul and with all your strength.*

*³⁷Jesus replied: "**Love the Lord your God** with all your heart and with all your soul and with all your mind."*

The Sadducees and Pharisees got together in **verse 34** of **Matthew Chapter 22**, and one of them, an expert in the law, tested our Lord Jesus Christ with the question: Teacher, which is the greatest commandment in the Law? Our Lord Jesus Christ answered: **"Love the Lord your God with all your heart and with all your soul and with all your mind."**

Now the question, how does the topic of this chapter—*Do you love God*?—apply to you? The question has four components amongst many others.

The first component is **Submission**, followed by **Obedience**. But perhaps even more significant is the desire and **Eagerness to please** the person or entity we profess to love so as to make them happy. The fourth component is **Delightfulness**. When you love a person or an entity, you will find that you are always delighted to be in their presence.

In applying the above four components to your relationship with our LORD God almighty, the following are the questions you will need to answer:

1. Do I **submit** to our LORD God almighty?

2. Do I **obey** the teachings of our LORD God almighty and His Son Jesus Christ?

3. Do I experience a **strong eagerness to please** our LORD God almighty at all times, whether or not I have received answers to my prayers?

4. Am I **delighted to be in His presence?** For example, when I am in Church, or during Bible Study classes and more importantly when I am alone in my quiet time of prayer and without anyone else present.

I once listened to a sermon where the Pastor made a statement that our LORD God almighty does not answer prayers. My stomach boiled and coiled at the statement with anger and distress as I wondered in my spirit, "How dare you make such a statement?" and "Who do you think you are?". He repeated the statement about three times and by the third time, even more emphatically, following which he then said, "**God answers the person praying with Yes and Amen, but not necessarily the prayer**". It was a wow moment as the penny dropped when the significance of the statement dawned on me. Thus the question: Does our LORD God almighty know you? **Do you have a relationship with Him**? Do you have the Holy Spirit resident in you?

But the man who loves God is known by God.

<u>*1 Corinthians 8: 3*</u>

*[7]And when you pray, do not keep on babbling like pagans because of their many words. [8]Do not be like them, **for your Father knows what you need before you ask him**."*

<u>*Matthew 6: 7-8*</u>

Have you ever wondered what our Lord Jesus Christ meant when he made the statement that our LORD God almighty knows your needs before you ask Him? The answer is quite simple. The **Holy Spirit** is the third entity of the **Trinity** that comprises God, Jesus, and the Holy Spirit. Hence, **if our LORD God almighty in the person of the Holy Spirit dwells in you, how would He not know your needs before you ask Him?**

Of course you cannot ask anything willy-nilly because whatever you ask of Him must be in accordance with His will and in line with the scriptures as written in *1 John 5: 14-15,* which is repeated below.

*¹⁴This is the confidence we have in approaching God: that if we ask anything according to **His will, he hears us.** ¹⁵And if we know that He hears us— whatever we ask—we know that we have what we asked of Him.*

John 5: 14-15

But perhaps the most significant way in which we are able to demonstrate our love for our LORD God almighty is through our act of **Obedience.** Disobedience is one of the biggest problems of humanity, whether the person is male or female, believer or unbeliever.

The reason is because **our act of disobedience started sadly from the very beginning of creation with Adam and Eve** and it has travelled down from generation to generation across the human race. When our LORD God almighty **specifically** told Adam and Eve not eat the forbidden fruit and both of them, irrespective of who deceived who, were recorded to have disobeyed the simple instruction of not to eat the fruit from one particular tree, whilst they were free to eat from every other tree in the garden of Eden.

Fast forward to today. Our Lord Jesus Christ instructed us **"not to worry",** four times in different forms between *Matthew 6: 25* and **33**. What do most of us do at the very first sign of distress? WE WORRY. Is that not disobedience?

*[25] "Therefore I tell you, **do not worry** about your life, what you will eat or drink; or about your body, what you will wear. Is not life more than food, and the body more than clothes?*

*[26]Look at the birds of the air; they do not sow or reap or store away in barns, and yet your heavenly Father feeds them. Are you not much more valuable than they? [27]Can any one of you by **worrying** add a single hour to your life? [28] "And **why do you worry** about clothes? See how the flowers of the field grow. They do not labour or spin. [29]Yet I tell you that not even Solomon in all his splendour was dressed like one of these. [30]If that is how God clothes the grass of the field, which is here today and tomorrow is thrown into the fire, will He not much more clothe you—you of little faith? [31]So **do not worry**, saying, 'What shall we eat?' or 'What shall we drink?' or 'What shall we wear?' [32]For the pagans run after all these things, and your heavenly Father knows that you need them. [33]But seek first his kingdom and his righteousness, and all these things will be given to you as well."*

Matthew 6: 25-33

Just imagine, if we cannot obey a simple instruction—**not to worry** but instead to trust our LORD God almighty completely (**Proverbs 3: 5**)—how then do we expect our prayers to be answered when most of the time all we do is engage in disobedience by worrying. Where then does **faith** come in? Is there any surprise why our Lord Jesus Christ questioned the faith of his disciples when they exhibited fear and desperation by waking him up in the boat because of a squall and fierce winds in **Mark 4: 35-41**. In *verse 40*, our Lord Jesus Christ challenged his disciples by asking them '**Why are you so afraid? Do you still have no faith?'**

Still on obedience, our Lord Jesus Christ stated again in **Matthew 7:21** that:

*[21]Not everyone who says to me, 'Lord, Lord', will enter the kingdom of heaven, **but only he who does the will of my Father** who is in heaven.*

Sadly many believers still do not understand what it means to love God as they simply argue that they go to church regularly and also engage in doing good things like giving to charitable causes. Trust me, that is very good and truly commendable and you will surely receive your rewards as our Lord Jesus Christ says so. But then, does that equate to loving God with all your heart, all your soul, and all your mind? Our Lord Jesus Christ gave us a good insight into how to demonstrate our genuine love for our LORD God almighty.

The teachings of our Lord Jesus Christ in **John 14** and **15** are very instructive.

*15If you love me, **you will obey** what I command. 16And I will ask the Father and He will give you another Counsellor to be with you for ever—the Spirit of truth.*

John 14: 15-17

*7If you **abide** in me and my words **abide** in you, **ask whatever you wish, and it will be given you.** 8This is to my Father's glory, that you bear much fruit, showing yourselves to be my disciples.*

John 15: 7-8

The Essence of 'Obedience'

The significance of obedience in our Christian walk cannot be over-emphasised as every aspect of our relationship with the LORD God almighty and His Son Jesus Christ **rests on it**.

Just imagine a scenario where your son or daughter comes to you and tells you, Dad/Mum, you know what, I love you very much because you have been there for me since my birth. You have provided for me, you have cared for my needs, and whenever I have taken ill, you have looked after me and nursed me back to full health. You have clothed me and ensured that I have a roof over my head and food to eat to nourish me all through my growing up years. I just love you very much Dad/Mum and promise to always **obey** you and do things that will please you and give you joy, so that whenever you think about me, you will confidently say, this is my beloved son or daughter in whom I am well pleased. I am confident that 100% of Fathers and Mothers reading this book will says yes, as they will be very delighted indeed to have such a son or daughter and also be willing to do much more for him or her in order to make the child very happy.

It is exactly the same way our LORD God almighty feels when we obey his teachings and abide in His Son, our Lord and Saviour Jesus Christ, whom He sent into the world for our salvation. **If our LORD God almighty can say the same about His Son Jesus Christ, can He say the same about you that this is my beloved Son or Daughter in whom I am well pleased?**

The blessings that are associated with loving our LORD God almighty with all our heart, soul, and mind are immense and cannot be encapsulated in just a few words. Hence, I will simply throw light on them with a number of scripture passages; it would not be what I say but instead what the scriptures say.

*[28]And we know that in all things **God works for the good of those who love Him**, who have been called according to His purpose.*

Romans 8: 28

*[9]However, as it is written: **"No eye has seen, no ear has heard, no mind has conceived** what God has prepared **for those who love Him"** [10]but God has revealed it to us by His Spirit.*

1 Corinthians 2: 9-10

*[2]We know we love God's children if we love God and **obey** His commandments. [3]**Loving God means keeping His commandments**, and HIS commandments are not burdensome.*

1 John 5: 2-3

[14]*"Because **he loves me**," says the LORD, "I will rescue him; I will protect him, for he acknowledges my name.* [15]*He will call on me, and I will answer him; I will be with him in trouble, I will deliver him and honour him.* [16]*With long life I will satisfy him and show him my salvation.*

<u>Psalm 91: 14-16</u>

In **John 21: 15-17** our Lord Jesus Christ asked Peter thrice: '**Do you love me?'**

[15]*When they had finished eating, Jesus said to Simon Peter, "Simon son of John, **do you love me** more than these?" "Yes, Lord," he said, "you know that I love you." Jesus said, "Feed my lambs."*

[16]*Again Jesus said, "Simon son of John, **do you love me**?" He answered, "Yes, Lord, you know that I love you." Jesus said, "Take care of my sheep."*

[17]*The third time he said to him, "Simon son of John, **do you love me**?" Peter was hurt because Jesus asked him the third time, "Do you love me?" He said, "Lord, you know all things; you know that I love you." Jesus said, "Feed my sheep."*

<u>John 21: 15-17</u>

CHAPTER 11

The Certainty of the Uncertain

*¹³Enter through the narrow gate. For wide is the gate and broad is the road that leads to destruction, and many enter through it. ¹⁴But small is the gate and narrow the road that leads to life, and **only a few find** it.*

Matthew 7: 13-14

Apart from death, one of the very few things in life that is certain is that nothing is certain. Not even the fact that a person will sleep and wake up the next morning.

I know a man whose mother went to bed about 52 years ago and sadly she was gone before the next morning. She was 45 years old. The same man's father-in-law went to bed, almost 36 years ago in very good health, and sadly, he passed on during the night. He was 49 years old. To compound matters, one of his brothers was having a chat with two of his friends in his office when he suddenly slumped and before anyone knew what was happening, he was gone. He was only 40 years old. Ironically, that is the reality of living. Nothing else is certain, yet sadly, death is certain for every man and woman at one stage or the other in their journey of life. That is, when the person reaches the terminus of his or her life.

Why is this poignant description of the uncertainty of what is surely certain? None of us know when we will hear the last call. It brings to mind the story of the rich man in the Holy Bible who after gathering his barn together decided to settle down and enjoy his wealth. That was when our LORD God almighty told him that his life will be demanded from him that very night (*Luke 12:15-21*). See also *James 4: 14*.

¹⁵*Then he said to them, "Watch out! Be on your guard against all kinds of greed;* **life does not consist in an abundance of possessions.***"* ¹⁶*And he told them this parable: "The ground of a certain rich man yielded an abundant harvest.* ¹⁷*He thought to himself, 'What shall I do? I have no place to store my crops.'* ¹⁸*Then he said, 'This is what I'll do. I will tear down my barns and build bigger ones, and there I will store my surplus grain.* ¹⁹*And I'll say to myself, "You have plenty of grain laid up for many years. Take life easy; eat, drink and be merry."'* ²⁰**But God said to him, 'You fool! This very night your life will be demanded from you.** *Then who will get what you have prepared for yourself?'* ²¹*This is how it will be with whoever stores up things for themselves but is not rich toward God."*

Luke 12: 15-21

¹⁴*Why, you do not even know what will happen tomorrow. What is your life? You are a mist that appears for a little while and then vanishes.*

James 4: 14

The end of life is so uncertain; we all know for sure that the unavoidable day will come and that each day when we wake up, we are reminded that we are one day closer to our last day on earth. Do you then not wonder if today happens to be your last day on earth? **Are you prepared for what comes next**?

I was discussing this point with my son some time ago as to why I chose to give my life to our Lord Jesus Christ. I told him that supposing I die now and then find out that heaven exists after all and that our Lord Jesus Christ has indeed prepared a mansion for me as He promised in **John 14: 1-3,** would it not be wonderful? **What then would I have lost**?

Absolutely nothing, as I would have gained eternity with our LORD God almighty and His precious Son, our Lord Jesus Christ.

On the other hand, if I choose not to bother about God and the teachings of our Lord Jesus Christ whilst on earth and when my time here ends and I get to the other side only to realise that hell in fact exists and that it is just as our Lord Jesus Christ described it in *Rev. 20: 14-15*, a place of pain and suffering with people crying in the lake of fire, **what would I have lost**?

Absolutely everything, as I may have enjoyed the pleasures that the sinful flesh had to offer whilst on planet earth only to trade it thereafter for the second death in the lake of fire with satan and his cohorts of evil doers. What a great loss that would then be.

*14 Then death and Hades were thrown into the lake of fire. The **lake of fire is the second death**. 15 Anyone whose name was not found written in the book of life was thrown into the lake of fire.*

Rev. 20: 14-15

The choice is simple. If you have not made it already, then you can make it today as your read these pages. **What do I have to do, you ask me.** Four very simple steps:

1. Repent from your life sins genuinely. Our LORD God almighty likes a contrite and penitent heart. Such He does not despise.

16 You do not delight in sacrifice, or I would bring it; you do not take pleasure in burnt offerings. 17 The sacrifices of God are a broken spirit; a broken and contrite heart, O God, you will not despise.

Psalm 51: 16-17

2. Ask to be filtered, washed, and cleansed by the Holy Spirit of every sin and impurity that resides in you.

7 Cleanse me with hyssop, and I will be clean; wash me, and I will be whiter than snow.

Psalm 51: 7

3. Ask our LORD God almighty to teach you His ways just as Moses did. You can do this by reading the Holy Bible every day and the Word of our LORD God almighty will serve as a **beacon** for the **holy and righteous living** that you are called to live, even if it is one chapter a day. Pray for edification and help of the Holy Spirit as you read the Holy Bible.

[13]If you are pleased with me, teach me your ways so I may know you and continue to find favour with you ...

Exodus 33: 13

4. Asked to be **filled** and **empowered** by the **Holy Spirit** so that you can live a life that glorifies and honours our LORD God almighty and His precious Son, our Lord and Saviour Jesus Christ.

[8]But you will receive power when the Holy Spirit comes on you; and you will be my witnesses in Jerusalem, and in all Judea and Samaria, and to the ends of the earth.

Acts 1: 8

CHAPTER 12

Blessings for Obedience

For quite some time now, I have wrestled with the word **'WHY'**.

For example: **Why do so many believers suffer from all kinds of failings in their Christian walk?**

I attributed it to so many factors, which included ignorance, pride, greed, selfishness, fear, lust, and possibly several other factors. However, there was one factor that appeared to top the rest—**Disobedience**.

As we read in the chapter 10, our acts of disobedience started sadly from the very beginning of creation with Adam and Eve and it has cascaded down from generation to generation across the human race. In this chapter, whilst we look at examples of disobedience, our focus will be on the **blessings for obedience**. So, **what happens when we obey** the teachings and commands of our LORD God almighty and His precious Son, our Lord and Saviour Jesus Christ?

How It All Started: Adam and Eve

¹Now the serpent was more crafty than any of the wild animals the Lord God had made. He said to the woman, "Did God really say, 'You must not eat from any tree in the garden'?"

²The woman said to the serpent, "We may eat fruit from the trees in the garden, ³but God did say, 'You must not eat fruit from the tree that is in the middle of the garden, and you must not touch it, or you will die.'"

4"*You will not certainly die,*" *the serpent said to the woman.* 5"*For God knows that when you eat from it your eyes will be opened, and you will be like God, knowing good and evil.*"

6*When the woman saw that the fruit of the tree was good for food and pleasing to the eye, and also desirable for gaining wisdom, she took some and ate it. She also gave some to her husband, who was with her, and he ate it.*

7*Then the eyes of both of them were opened, and they realized they were naked; so they sewed fig leaves together and made coverings for themselves.*

8*Then the man and his wife heard the sound of the Lord God as he was walking in the garden in the cool of the day, and they hid from the Lord God among the trees of the garden.*

9*But the Lord God called to the man, "Where are you?"*

10*He answered, "I heard you in the garden, and I was afraid because I was naked; so I hid."*

11*And he said, "Who told you that you were naked? Have you eaten from the tree that I commanded you not to eat from?"*

12*The man said, "The woman you put here with me—she gave me some fruit from the tree, and I ate it."*

13*Then the Lord God said to the woman, "What is this you have done?" The woman said, "The serpent deceived me, and I ate."*

Genesis 3: 1-13

I will not go into the intricacies of who did what or who is to blame from the above story. The key message that I wish to highlight by sharing the story in this book is the message of **disobedience, which sadly has consequences**.

Saul and the Amalekites

Now let us fast forward and look at the story of Saul who was instructed by God to go and totally destroy the Amalekites as punishment for waylaying the children of Israel when they came up from Egypt.

The instruction God gave Saul was specific in that he was not to spare anyone or their flocks. What did Saul do, he spared the life of Agag, king of the Amalekites, as well as the best of their sheep and cattle, the fat calves and the lambs, everything that was good.

Below is the reaction of Samuel when word about what Saul did got to him:

*22But Samuel replied: "Does the LORD delight in burnt offerings and sacrifices as much as in **obeying** the LORD? To **obey** is better than sacrifice, and to heed is better than the fat of rams. 23For rebellion is like the sin of divination, and arrogance like the evil of idolatry. Because you have rejected the word of the LORD, he has **rejected** you as king"*

1 Samuel 15: 22-23

Now, let us look at what happens when we obey the teachings and commands of our LORD God almighty.

Blessings for Obedience from Old Testament

1If you fully obey the Lord your God and carefully follow all his commands I give you today, the Lord your God will set you high above all the nations on earth.

2All these blessings will come on you and accompany you if you obey the Lord your God:

3You will be blessed in the city and blessed in the country.

4The fruit of your womb will be blessed, and the crops of your land and the young of your livestock—the calves of your herds and the lambs of your flocks.

5Your basket and your kneading trough will be blessed.

6You will be blessed when you come in and blessed when you go out.

⁷The Lord will grant that the enemies who rise up against you will be defeated before you. They will come at you from one direction but flee from you in seven.

⁸The Lord will send a blessing on your barns and on everything you put your hand to. The Lord your God will bless you in the land he is giving you.

⁹The Lord will establish you as his holy people, as he promised you on oath, if you keep the commands of the Lord your God and walk in obedience to him.

¹⁰Then all the peoples on earth will see that you are called by the name of the Lord, and they will fear you.

¹¹The Lord will grant you abundant prosperity—in the fruit of your womb, the young of your livestock and the crops of your ground—in the land he swore to your ancestors to give you.

¹²The Lord will open the heavens, the storehouse of his bounty, to send rain on your land in season and to bless all the work of your hands. You will lend to many nations but will borrow from none.

¹³The Lord will make you the head, not the tail. If you pay attention to the commands of the Lord your God that I give you this day and carefully follow them, you will always be at the top, never at the bottom.

¹⁴Do not turn aside from any of the commands I give you today, to the right or to the left, following other gods and serving them.

Deuteronomy 28: 1-14

Blessings for Obedience from New Testament

In addition to the blessings highlighted above, one key blessing which far outweighs the blessings listed in **Deuteronomy 28: 1-14** is that of the **Holy Spirit**. In **Act 5: 32**, Peter stated categorically that **the Holy Spirit is given to those who obey our LORD God almighty**. Thus, despite the persecution that the Apostles faced after the crucifixion of our Lord Jesus Christ, which included imprisonments, floggings, public harassments, and humiliations, Peter wrote:

[29]But Peter and the other apostles replied: **We must obey God rather than men**. *[30]The God of our ancestors raised Jesus from the dead, whom you killed by hanging him on a cross. [31]God exalted him to his right hand as Prince and Saviour that he might give repentance and forgive their sins. [32]We are witnesses of these things,* **and so is the Holy Spirit, whom God has given to those who obey him**.

Acts 5: 29-32

The decision of Peter and his fellow disciples **to obey God** rather than men, which he further emphasised by his affirmative statement in *verse 32,* **in that our LORD God almighty gives the Holy Spirit to those who obey Him, should be given very close attention.** This was emphasised upon by our Lord Jesus:

*[15]***"If you love me, obey my commandments**. *[16]And I will ask the Father, and he will give you another Advocate,* **who will never leave you**. *[17]***He is the Holy Spirit**, *who leads into all truth..."*

John 14: 15-17

The blessings for obedience whether in the old testament or the new testament is **transformative and life changing**. Hence, I urge every believer and non-believer reading this book to reflect and pay particular attention to the essence and importance of **obedience** when it comes to the teachings and commands of our LORD God almighty and His precious Son, our Lord and Saviour Jesus Christ, **as it will open the door that allows each person to experience the Kingdom of God that is here and now.**

[20]Once, on being asked by the Pharisees when the Kingdom of God would come, Jesus replied, "The coming of the Kingdom of God is not something that can be observed, [21]nor will people say, 'Here it is,' or 'There it is,' **because the Kingdom of God is within you**.*"*

Luke 17: 20-21

CHAPTER 13

Earth or Eternity
What are you preparing for?

The topic of this chapter could easily be misunderstood, as it gives the impression that it would only cover matters concerning eternity but probably ignore the period we are meant to spend on earth. That may, in fact, be far from the truth. You can live your life to the full on earth and still enjoy eternity with our Lord Jesus Christ and the LORD God almighty.

Our Lord Jesus Christ taught us as follows:

10' The thief does not come except to steal, and to kill, and to destroy; I have come that they may have life, and that they may have it more abundantly'.

John 10: 10

Hence, from the time you were born and till the time you transition into eternity, **how do you intend to live your life?** Do you want to live your life for yourself or in a manner that honours and glorifies our LORD God almighty and His precious Son our Lord Jesus Christ?

As you read this chapter, may I ask you a simple question: Do you desire to live your life to the full whilst on earth and still make heaven in order to spend eternity with our Lord Jesus Christ when your time on earth comes to an end? If your answer is yes, the next question is: How do you do that? That is, how to live your life to the full on earth and thereafter enjoy eternity with our Lord Jesus Christ?

Be Born Again

*'I tell you the truth, no-one can see the kingdom of God **unless he is born again'**.*

John 3: 3

The usual reaction to this statement from believers is: 'But I am already a Christian and I attend church services regularly. Hence, why do I still need to be born again?' The answer is simple. Have you **given** your life to our Lord Jesus Christ? Are you **filled** with the Holy Spirit? And are you **yielded** to the Holy Spirit?

Our Lord Jesus Christ further taught us as follows:

*⁶'I am **the way and the truth and the life**. No-one comes to the Father except through me'.*

John 14: 6

The reality is that just because you have been attending church services for more than 30 years is not necessarily an indication of a life lived in **holiness** and **righteousness**. The truth is that being **born again** has nothing to do with how long you have been a Christian. Rather, **the point is, are you in Church or in Christ**?

Salvation is not about being active in Church. It is not determined by whether you play multiple roles in Church, but rather about whether you are born again, filled with the Holy Spirit and completely yielded to the Holy Spirit and manifesting his fruits in your home, your work place, your school, on the playground, your university, in the market place and of course in your church amongst your Kingdom brothers and sisters.

Live a Sacrificial Life

[24]If anyone would come after me, he must deny himself and take up his cross and follow me. [25]For whoever wants to save his life will lose it, but whoever loses his life for me will find it. [26]What good would it be for a man if he gains the whole world, yet forfeits his soul? Or what can a man give in exchange for his soul?

Matthew 16: 24-26

As believers, we are meant to live a life that is Christ-focused and not necessarily self-focused. In other words, we are meant to live our lives in an altruistic manner that is devoid of psychological egoism. When we focus on ourselves, we will be selfish; but when we focus on our Lord Jesus Christ, we will be selfless.

It explains why our Lord Jesus Christ further admonished us on the point when he told us:

[19]'Do not store up for yourselves treasures on earth, where moth and rust destroy, and where thieves break in and steal. [20]But store up for yourselves treasures in heaven, where moth and rust do not destroy, and where thieves do not break in and steal. [21]For where your treasure is, there your heart will be also.'

Matthew 6: 19-21

Please note that living a life of selflessness should not be misconstrued that Christians should not aspire to be successful and prosperous in life. That is not the intention. For example, most of us desire good things for ourselves and our families. We pray for good schools for our children and also good careers for them when they finish university. There is nothing wrong with such desires and prayers. Of course, when you are Christ-focused and at the same time successful in your careers and businesses, you will not need anyone to tell you to generously support Kingdom expansion efforts on earth because you will do it gleefully as our LORD God almighty loves a cheerful giver.

⁷Each of you should give what you have decided in your heart to give, not reluctantly or under compulsion, for God loves a cheerful giver.

2 Corinthians 9: 7

As a matter of fact, **material and worldly things will not even interest you that much, because you will be more interested in extending God's work on earth,** as such actions helps to bring salvation to many homes and spiritual deliverance to many families.

Have Complete Faith in God

⁶'And without faith it is impossible to please God, because anyone who comes to Him must believe that He exists and that He rewards those who earnestly seek Him'.

Hebrews 11: 6

When the disciples could not heal a child that was suffering from seizures, our Lord Jesus Christ told his disciples as follows:

²⁰'Because you have so little faith. I tell you the truth, if you have faith as small as a mustard seed, you can say to this mountain, "Move from here to there," and it will move. Nothing will be impossible for you.'

Matthew 17: 20

Bear Fruit

If you are familiar with the parable of the Sower, you will remember what happened to the seed that fell on good soil. In **Matthew 13:23** our Lord Jesus Christ said, 'But the one who received the seed that fell on good soil is the man who hears the word and understands it. He produces a crop, yielding a hundred, sixty, or thirty times what was sown'.

*5'I am the vine; you are the branches. If a man remains in me and I in him, he will bear much fruit; apart from me you can do nothing. 7If you remain in me and my words remain in you, ask whatever you wish, and it will be given you. 8**This is to my Father's glory that you bear much fruit**, showing yourselves to be my disciples.'*

<u>John 15: 5,7-8</u>

Now, after all said and done, **what are you preparing for: Earth or eternity?** If you are not yet born again, then it is obvious that you have to be born again in order to see and experience the Kingdom of God even whilst you are still on planet earth. Our time here on earth may be short or long, but compared to eternity, there really is no basis for comparison. Hence, I urge you my brothers and sisters in Christ to **yield** to the Holy Spirit and live your lives for Christ. It represents an **investment for eternity with our Lord Jesus Christ.**

22Do not merely listen to the word, and so deceive yourselves. Do what it says. 23Any one who listens to the word but does not do what it says is like someone who looks at his face in a mirror 24and, after looking at himself, goes away and immediately forgets what he looks like.

<u>James 1:22-24</u>

It is my fervent prayer that when our time on earth comes to an end, every believer who has been blessed to read this book will make heaven and spend eternity with our LORD God almighty in the mighty name of Jesus Christ, amen.

CHAPTER 14

Where are you with Christ?

The Parable of the Sower

¹That same day Jesus went out of the house and sat by the lake.

²Such large crowds gathered around him that he got into a boat and sat in it, while all the people stood on the shore.

³Then he told them many things in parables, saying: "A farmer went out to sow his seed.

⁴As he was scattering the seed, some fell along the path, and the birds came and ate it up.

⁵Some fell on rocky places, where it did not have much soil. It sprang up quickly, because the soil was shallow.

⁶But when the sun came up, the plants were scorched, and they withered because they had no root.

⁷Other seed fell among thorns, which grew up and choked the plants.

⁸Still other seed fell on good soil, where it produced a crop—a hundred, sixty, or thirty times what was sown.

⁹Whoever has ears, let them hear."

¹⁰The disciples came to him and asked, "Why do you speak to the people in parables?"

¹¹He replied, "Because the knowledge of the secrets of the kingdom of heaven has been given to you, but not to them.

¹²Whoever has will be given more, and they will have an abundance. Whoever does not have, even what they have will be taken from them.

¹³*This is why I speak to them in parables:*

'Though seeing, they do not see; though hearing, they do not hear or understand.

¹⁴*In them is fulfilled the prophecy of Isaiah: "You will be ever hearing but never understanding; you will be ever seeing but never perceiving."'*

¹⁵*For this people's heart has become calloused; they hardly hear with their ears, and they have closed their eyes. Otherwise they might see with their eyes, hear with their ears, understand with their hearts and turn, and I would heal them.*

¹⁶*But blessed are your eyes because they see, and your ears because they hear.*

¹⁷*For truly I tell you, many prophets and righteous people longed to see what you see but did not see it, and to hear what you hear but did not hear it.*

¹⁸**Listen then to what the parable of the Sower means:**

¹⁹*When anyone hears the message about the kingdom and **does not understand it**, the evil one comes and snatches away what was sown in their heart. This is the seed sown along the path.*

²⁰*The seed falling on rocky ground refers to someone who hears the word and at once receives it with joy.*

²¹*But since **they have no root**, they last only a short time. When trouble or persecution comes because of the word, they quickly fall away.*

²²*The seed falling among the thorns refers to someone who hears the word, but the **worries of this life and the deceitfulness of wealth** choke the word, making it unfruitful.*

²³*But the seed falling on good soil refers to someone who **hears the word and understands it**. This is the one who **produces a crop**, yielding a hundred, sixty or thirty times what was sown."*

Matthew 13: 1-23

The parable of the Sower is one of those parables that teaches us to ask the following questions of ourselves to assess **where we are in our relationship with our Lord Jesus Christ.**

1. Am I a seed that fell along the path?
2. Am I a seed that fell on the rock?
3. Am I a seed that fell among the thorns?
4. Am I a seed that fell on good soil?

It is evident from the scriptures that the only place to be is on good soil, where you can produce souls for Christ in their hundreds, sixties, and thirties. The next question therefore is:

5. Why am I where I am with Christ today?

Some of you reading this book may safely conclude that they are already on good soil and yielding souls for Christ. That is a very good thing and I say well done.

However, the question is for those who in their hearts know that they are definitely not yet on good soil. If that is you, then why are you not on good soil? That is, **what currently prevents you from being on good soil and yielding souls for Christ** in the hundreds, sixties, and thirties?

Could it be **Ignorance; Fear; Doubt; Unbelief; Disobedience; Lack of Faith; Unanswered Prayers; Depression; Adultery and Fornication; Indebtedness; Internet Pornography; Nudity on Television; Homosexuality; or Godless and devil-inspired Television and the mainstream Press**?

I don't know where you are with Christ at this moment in your life, but in your heart, you know where you are. The next question then is:

6. What do I need to do in order to yield souls for Christ?

The **first step** is to **repent** and **confess your sins**. The scriptures state:

⁷"I tell you that in the same way there will be more rejoicing in heaven over one sinner who repents than over ninety-nine righteous persons who do not need to repent."

Luke 15: 7

⁹"If we confess our sins, He is faithful and righteous to forgive us our sins and to cleanse us from all unrighteousness."

1 John 1: 9

The **second step** is to **yield to the Holy Spirit** and **surrender your life to Jesus Christ**. In *John 3: 3*, our Lord Jesus Christ declared: *'I tell you the truth, no one can see the kingdom of God unless he is born again'*. If there is one thing that remains without question, it is your need to be born again and receive the Holy Spirit. To be fruitful for Christ, you have to be **filled** with the **Holy Spirit**. And to serve our Lord Jesus Christ, you must be born again.

The **third step** is to **trust our LORD God almighty completely** and allow the **Holy Spirit** to **guide, equip,** and **bless** you with the **spiritual tools** you require to be **fruitful** for Christ. In *John 14: 15-17,* our Lord Jesus Christ said: *'If you love me, you will obey what I command. And I will ask the Father and He will give you another Counsellor to be with you for ever—the **Spirit of truth**. The world cannot accept him, because it neither sees him nor knows him. But you know him, for he lives with you and will be in you'.*

The **fourth step** is for you to be **salt of the earth** and **light of the world** (*Matthew 5:13-16*). This can sometimes be seen as very difficult to achieve. I can assure you that you cannot do it on your own with just human effort. The scriptures taught us in *Philippians 4: 13*: *'I can do everything through Him who gives me strength'.* This is a very important step because whether we like it or not, people are watching us and the best way to lead others to Christ is by being salt of the earth and light of the world. The way we live our lives should serve as **good testimony** for our Lord Jesus Christ.

The **fifth and final step** is to be a **witness for our Lord Jesus Christ** and **share your faith confidently with others** at every opportunity. This step is sometimes described as one of the most daunting steps to take as a Christian. How does one witness for Christ, for example, in the western world, without being accused of stepping on other people's toes or causing offence.

In today's world of political correctness and multi-faith Britain (where I reside), how can a Christian fulfil the command of the 'Great Commission'?

19"Therefore go and make disciples of all nations, baptising them in the name of the Father 20and of the Son and of the Holy Spirit and teaching them to obey everything I have commanded."

Matthew 28: 19-20

If you are still asking yourself the question of whether or not you fell on good soil, now is the moment of truth.

In the parable of the **Wise and Foolish Builders** our Lord Jesus Christ was very clear when he said:

*24'Therefore everyone who **hears these words of mine and puts them into practice is like a wise man who built his house on the rock.** 25The rain came down, the streams rose, and the winds blew and beat against that house; yet it did not fall, because it had its foundations on the rock.*

26But everyone who hears these words of mine and does not put them into practice is like a foolish man who built his house on sand. 27The rain came down, the streams rose, and the winds blew and beat against that house, and it fell with a great crash'.

Matthew 7: 24-27

It is my fervent prayer that the message in this chapter helps you to reflect on where you are with our Lord Jesus Christ and to reset your priorities going forward, so that you can ensure that you are on good soil (if you are not already there) and yielding souls in their hundreds, sixties, and thirties for our LORD God almighty in the mighty name of Jesus Christ, amen.

CHAPTER 15

When God Intervenes

This chapter deals with the transformational influence of the intervention of God in our lives. **When our LORD God almighty intervenes in our lives, the natural becomes supernatural, whilst the ordinary becomes extra-ordinary**.

When God intervenes in our lives, our abilities and capacities to witness takes a new turn, and our Kingdom service moves from ordinary exploits to extra-ordinary exploits. **This results in a release of power and enablement that propels the believer to do things that would otherwise not have been deemed possible for ordinary human beings.** For example, Sarah gave birth to Isaac at the age of 90; Moses was saved from certain death as a child; the Israelites walked through the Red Sea on dry land; Joseph effectively became the Prime Minister of Egypt straight from prison; the wall of Jericho fell after the Israelites walked around it for seven days; David, the shepherd boy, defeated the mighty Goliath; Meshach, Shadrach, and Abednego survived the blazing furnace; Daniel slept all night with lions and survived unscathed; whilst our Lord Jesus Christ walked on water and also rose from death after three days.

The common assumption is that the intervention of our LORD God almighty should represent abundant blessings that takes away afflictions, challenges, difficulties, sorrow and harrowing deaths. Ironically, the reality is much different as what usually precedes His intervention may be challenging events and His intervention then appears to be a form of rescue. It could be the other way round or a mixture of both, as was the case with Job. **God's intervention in our lives is for His purposes to be fulfilled for humanity and not necessarily for the purpose of us having big houses, big cars, fat bank accounts, and big church buildings, as some Christian leaders would make us believe.**

The irony that comes with the intervention of God is that we are also empowered to cope with a level of adversity, pain, and loss, including harrowing deaths, without losing our faith and focus on who we are in Christ, which again would otherwise not have been possible. Case in point are the harrowing deaths of most of the twelve apostles of our Lord Jesus Christ, and also Paul, despite the beatings and his many near death experiences.

In this chapter, I am simply going to highlight the lives of eight people on six different occasions in the Bible and use it to demonstrate what happens when our Father in Heaven intervenes in our lives. Let us start with Abraham.

Abraham

¹The Lord had said to Abram, "Go from your country, your people and your father's household to the land I will show you. ²I will make you into a great nation, and I will bless you; I will make your name great, and you will be a blessing. ³I will bless those who bless you, and whoever curses you I will curse; and all peoples on earth will be blessed through you."

Genesis 12: 1-3

¹After this, the word of the Lord came to Abram in a vision: "Do not be afraid, Abram. I am your shield, your very great reward." ²But Abram said, "Sovereign Lord, what can you give me since I remain childless and the one who will inherit my estate is Eliezer of Damascus?" ³And Abram said, "You have given me no children; so a servant in my household will be my heir."

⁴Then the word of the Lord came to him: "This man will not be your heir, but a son who is your own flesh and blood will be your heir." ⁵He took him outside and said, "Look up at the sky and count the stars—if indeed you can count them." Then he said to him, "So shall your offspring be." ⁶Abram believed the Lord, and he credited it to him as righteousness.

<u>Genesis 15: 1-6</u>

*¹The Lord appeared to Abraham near the great trees of Mamre while he was sitting at the entrance to his tent in the heat of the day. ²Abraham looked up and saw three men standing nearby. When he saw them, he hurried from the entrance of his tent to meet them and bowed low to the ground. ³He said, "If I have found favour in your eyes, my lord, do not pass your servant by. ⁴Let a little water be brought, and then you may all wash your feet and rest under this tree. ⁵Let me get you something to eat, so you can be refreshed and then go on your way—now that you have come to your servant." "Very well," they answered, "do as you say." ⁶So Abraham hurried into the tent to Sarah. "Quick," he said, "get three seahs of the finest flour and knead it and bake some bread." ⁷Then he ran to the herd and selected a choice, tender calf and gave it to a servant, who hurried to prepare it. ⁸He then brought some curds and milk and the calf that had been prepared, and set these before them. While they ate, he stood near them under a tree. ⁹"Where is your wife Sarah?" they asked him. "There, in the tent," he said. ¹⁰Then one of them said, "I will surely return to you about this time next year, and Sarah your wife will have a son." Now Sarah was listening at the entrance to the tent, which was behind him. ¹¹Abraham and Sarah were already very old, and Sarah was past the age of childbearing. ¹²So Sarah laughed to herself as she thought, "After I am worn out and my lord is old, will I now have this pleasure?" ¹³Then the LORD said to Abraham, "Why did Sarah laugh and say, 'Will I really have a child, now that I am old?' ¹⁴**Is anything too hard for the LORD?** I will return to you at the **appointed time** next year, and Sarah will have a son." ¹⁵Sarah was afraid, so she lied and said, "I did not laugh." But he said, "Yes, you did laugh."*

<u>Genesis 18: 1-15</u>

Joseph

*37The plan seemed good to Pharaoh and to all his officials. 38So Pharaoh asked them, "Can we find anyone like this man, **one in whom is the spirit of God**?" 39Then Pharaoh said to Joseph, "Since God has made all this known to you, there is no one so discerning and wise as you. 40You shall be in charge of my palace, and all my people are to submit to your orders. Only with respect to the throne will I be greater than you." 41So Pharaoh said to Joseph, "I hereby put you in charge of the whole land of Egypt." 42Then Pharaoh took his signet ring from his finger and put it on Joseph's finger. He dressed him in robes of fine linen and put a gold chain around his neck. 43He had him ride in a chariot as his second-in-command, and people shouted before him, "Make way!" Thus he put him in charge of the whole land of Egypt. 44Then Pharaoh said to Joseph, "I am Pharaoh, but without your word no one will lift hand or foot in all Egypt." 45Pharaoh gave Joseph the name Zaphenath-Paneah and gave him Asenath daughter of Potiphera, priest of On, to be his wife. And Joseph went throughout the land of Egypt. 46Joseph was thirty years old when he entered the service of Pharaoh king of Egypt. And Joseph went out from Pharaoh's presence and travelled throughout Egypt.*

Genesis 41: 37-46

Moses

*1Now a man of the tribe of Levi married a Levite woman, 2and she became pregnant and gave birth to a son. When she saw that he was a fine child, she hid him for three months. 3But when she could hide him no longer, she got a papyrus basket for him and coated it with tar and pitch. Then she placed the child in it and put it among the reeds along the bank of the Nile. 4His sister stood at a distance to see what would happen to him. 5Then Pharaoh's daughter went down to the Nile to bathe, and her attendants were walking along the riverbank. She saw the basket among the reeds and sent her female slave to get it. 6She opened it and saw the baby. He was crying, and she felt sorry for him. "This is one of the Hebrew babies," she said. 7Then his sister asked Pharaoh's daughter, "Shall I go and get one of the Hebrew women to nurse the baby for you?" 8"Yes, go," she answered. So the girl went and got the baby's mother. 9Pharaoh's daughter said to her, "**Take this*** *baby and nurse him for me, and I will pay you." So the woman took the baby and nursed him. ¹⁰When the child grew older, she took him to Pharaoh's daughter and he became her son. She named him Moses, saying, "I drew him out of the water."*

Exodus 2: 1-10

David

⁶When they arrived, Samuel saw Eliab and thought, "Surely the Lord's anointed stands here before the Lord." ⁷But the Lord said to Samuel, "Do not consider his appearance or his height, for I have rejected him. The Lord does not look at the things people look at. People look at the outward appearance, but the Lord looks at the heart." ⁸Then Jesse called Abinadab and had him pass in front of Samuel. But Samuel said, "The Lord has not chosen this one either." ⁹Jesse then had Shammah pass by, but Samuel said, "Nor has the Lord chosen this one." ¹⁰Jesse had seven of his sons pass before Samuel, but Samuel said to him, "The Lord has not chosen these." ¹¹So he asked Jesse, "Are these all the sons you have?" "There is still the youngest," Jesse answered. "He is tending the sheep." Samuel said, "Send for him; we will not sit down until he arrives." ¹²So he sent for him and had him brought in. He was glowing with health and had a fine appearance and handsome features. Then the Lord said, "Rise and anoint him; this is the one." ¹³ So Samuel took the horn of oil and anointed him in the presence of his brothers, and from that day on the Spirit of the Lord came powerfully upon David. Samuel then went to Ramah.

1 Samuel 16: 6-13

³⁸Then Saul dressed David in his own tunic. He put a coat of armour on him and a bronze helmet on his head. ³⁹David fastened on his sword over the tunic and tried walking around, because he was not used to them. "I cannot go in these," he said to Saul, "because I am not used to them." So he took them off. ⁴⁰Then he took his staff in his hand, chose five smooth stones from the stream, put them in the pouch of his shepherd's bag and, with his sling in his hand, approached the Philistine. ⁴¹Meanwhile, the Philistine, with his shield bearer in front of him, kept coming closer to David. ⁴²He looked David over and saw that he was little more than a boy, glowing with health and handsome, and he despised him. ⁴³He said to David, "Am I a dog, that you come at me with sticks?" And the Philistine cursed David by his gods. ⁴⁴"Come here," he said, "and I'll give your flesh to the birds and the wild animals!" ⁴⁵David said to the Philistine, "You come against me with sword and spear and javelin, but I come against you in the name of the LORD Almighty, the God of the armies of Israel, whom you have defied. ⁴⁶This day the LORD will deliver you into my hands, and I'll strike you down and cut off your head. This very day I will give the carcasses of the Philistine army to the birds and the wild animals, and the whole world will know that there is a God in Israel. ⁴⁷All those gathered here will know that it is not by sword or spear that the LORD saves; for the battle is the LORD's, and he will give all of you into our hands." ⁴⁸As the Philistine moved closer to attack him, David ran quickly toward the battle line to meet him. ⁴⁹Reaching into his bag and taking out a stone, he slung it and struck the Philistine on the forehead. The stone sank into his forehead, and he fell face down on the ground. ⁵⁰So David triumphed over the Philistine with a sling and a stone; without a sword in his hand he struck down the Philistine and killed him. ⁵¹David ran and stood over him. He took hold of the Philistine's sword and drew it from the sheath. After he killed him, he cut off his head with the sword. When the Philistines saw that their hero was dead, they turned and ran.

1 Samuel 17: 38-51

Shadrach, Meshach, and Abednego

⁸At this time some astrologers came forward and denounced the Jews. ⁹They said to King Nebuchadnezzar, "May the king live forever! ¹⁰ Your Majesty has issued a decree that everyone who hears the sound of the horn, flute, zither, lyre, harp, pipe and all kinds of music must fall down and worship the image of gold, ¹¹ and that whoever does not fall down and worship will be thrown into a blazing furnace. ¹² But there are some Jews whom you have set over the affairs of the province of Babylon—**Shadrach, Meshach and Abednego—who pay no attention to you, Your Majesty. They neither serve your gods nor worship the image of gold you have set up.**" ¹³Furious with rage, Nebuchadnezzar summoned Shadrach, Meshach and Abednego. So these men were brought before the king, ¹⁴and Nebuchadnezzar said to them, "Is it true, Shadrach, Meshach and Abednego, that you do not serve

my gods or worship the image of gold I have set up? ¹⁵Now when you hear the sound of the horn, flute, zither, lyre, harp, pipe and all kinds of music, **if you are ready to fall down and worship the image I made, very good. But if you do not worship it, you will be thrown immediately into a blazing furnace***.*

Then what god will be able to rescue you from my hand?" ¹⁶Shadrach, Meshach and Abednego replied to him, "King Nebuchadnezzar, we do not need to defend ourselves before you in this matter. **¹⁷If we are thrown into the blazing furnace, the God we serve is able to deliver us from it, and he will deliver us from Your Majesty's hand. ¹⁸But even if he does not, we want you to know, Your Majesty, that we will not serve your gods or worship the image of gold you have set up."** *¹⁹Then Nebuchadnezzar was furious with Shadrach, Meshach and Abednego, and his attitude toward them changed.* **He ordered the furnace heated seven times hotter than usual** *²⁰and commanded some of the strongest soldiers in his army to tie up Shadrach, Meshach and Abednego and throw them into the blazing furnace. ²¹So these men, wearing their robes, trousers, turbans and other clothes, were bound and thrown into the blazing furnace. ²²The king's command was so urgent and the furnace so hot that the flames of the fire killed the soldiers who took up Shadrach, Meshach and Abednego, ²³and these three men, firmly tied, fell into the blazing furnace.* **²⁴Then King Nebuchadnezzar leaped to his feet in amazement and asked his advisers, "Weren't there three men that we tied up and threw into the fire?" They replied, "Certainly, Your Majesty." ²⁵He said, "Look! I see four men walking around in the fire, unbound and unharmed, and the fourth looks like a son of the gods."** *²⁶Nebuchadnezzar then approached the opening of the blazing furnace and shouted, "Shadrach, Meshach and Abednego, servants of the Most High God, come out! Come here!" So Shadrach, Meshach and Abednego came out of the fire, ²⁷and the satraps, prefects, governors and royal advisers crowded around them. They saw that the fire had not harmed their bodies, nor was a hair of their heads singed; their robes were not scorched, and there was no smell of fire on them. ²⁸Then Nebuchadnezzar said,* **"Praise be to the God of Shadrach, Meshach and Abednego, who has sent his angel and rescued his servants!** *They trusted in him and defied the king's command and were willing to give up their lives rather than serve or worship any god except their* own God. [29]*Therefore I decree that the people of any nation or language who say anything against the God of Shadrach, Meshach and Abednego be cut into pieces and their houses be turned into piles of rubble, for no other god can save in this way."* [30]*Then the king promoted Shadrach, Meshach and Abednego in the province of Babylon.*

Daniel 3: 8-30

Paul

[1]*Meanwhile, Saul was still breathing out murderous threats against the Lord's disciples. He went to the high priest* [2]*and asked him for letters to the synagogues in Damascus, so that if he found any there who belonged to the Way, whether men or women, he might take them as prisoners to Jerusalem.* [3]**As he neared Damascus on his journey, suddenly a light from heaven flashed around him.** [4]**He fell to the ground and heard a voice say to him, "Saul, Saul, why do you persecute me?"** [5]**"Who are you, Lord?" Saul asked. "I am Jesus, whom you are persecuting," he replied.** [6]**"Now get up and go into the city, and you will be told what you must do."** [7]*The men traveling with Saul stood there speechless; they heard the sound but did not see anyone.* [8]*Saul got up from the ground, but when he opened his eyes he could see nothing. So they led him by the hand into Damascus.* [9]*For three days he was blind, and did not eat or drink anything.* [10]*In Damascus there was a disciple named Ananias. The Lord called to him in a vision, "Ananias!"* "Yes, Lord," he answered. [11]*The Lord told him, "Go to the house of Judas on Straight Street and ask for a man from Tarsus named Saul, for he is praying.* [12]*In a vision he has seen a man named Ananias come and place his hands on him to restore his sight."* [13]*"Lord," Ananias answered, "I have heard many reports about this man and all the harm he has done to your holy people in Jerusalem.* [14]*And he has come here with authority from the chief priests to arrest all who call on your name."* [15]**But the Lord said to Ananias, "Go! This man is my chosen instrument to proclaim my name to the Gentiles and their kings and to the people of Israel.** [16]**I will show him how much he must suffer for my name."** [17]*Then Ananias went to the house and entered it. Placing his hands on Saul, he said,* **"Brother Saul, the Lord—Jesus, who appeared to you on the road as you were coming here—has sent me so that you may see again and be filled with the Holy Spirit."** [18]*Immediately,*

something like scales fell from Saul's eyes, and he could see again. He got up and was baptized, ¹⁹*and after taking some food, he regained his strength. Saul spent several days with the disciples in Damascus.* ²⁰**At once he began to preach in the synagogues that Jesus is the Son of God**. ²¹*All those who heard him were astonished and asked, "Isn't he the man who raised havoc in Jerusalem among those who call on this name? And hasn't he come here to take them as prisoners to the chief priests?"* ²²**Yet Saul grew more and more powerful and baffled the Jews living in Damascus by proving that Jesus is the Messiah.**

<u>*Acts 9: 1-22*</u>

CHAPTER 16

And Then What?

24Then Jesus said to his disciples, "Whoever wants to be my disciple must deny themselves and take up their cross and follow me. 25For whoever wants to save their life will lose it, but whoever loses their life for me will find it. 26 **What good will it be for someone to gain the whole world, yet forfeit their soul***? Or what can anyone give in exchange for their soul?*

Matthew 16: 24-26

It started with the vision whilst on my knees praying, of being gifted by our LORD God almighty with £50 billion pounds sterling. I suddenly found that I could buy virtually any house that I desired in the world and the LORD God almighty asked me: And then what? Again, I discovered that I could buy all the cars that I ever desired in the world. Once more, our LORD God almighty asked me: And then what? Finally, I realised that I could live all kinds of lifestyles that involved indulging my flesh and denying myself nothing as was the case with Solomon. Yes and again, our LORD God almighty asked me: And then what?

The teaching by our Lord Jesus Christ in **Matthew 16:26** is the crux of human living and existence. In essence, what is it that we are chasing in this world? Is it wealth? Is it beauty? Is it fame? Is it popularity? Is it a good career? Is it a big house or a big car? The key overarching question after we have attained our primary, secondary and ultimate goals in life is: And then what? **For most people what happens next is a life of indulgence, which ultimately leads to sin**

and perdition because the mind of man, the soul of man, and the inner man without the Holy Spirit is the playground for the devil.

Rather, **what should we do** when we receive exceptional blessings of abundant material, financial, intellectual or physical prosperity from our LORD God almighty? Simple. Such blessings provide us with the opportunity and privilege to serve our LORD God almighty by living our lives in humility and love for our fellow human beings as witnesses for our Lord Jesus Christ. The resources and blessings we receive from our Father in Heaven must be used for His Kingdom purposes. It is thus important to always remind ourselves that there is nothing that we have that we have not received, starting from our very own existence.

The breath that we have that enables us to function—yes, the oxygen that we breathe in every second—is a gift from our LORD God almighty. The food we eat, the good health we enjoy, the clothes we wear, the roof over our heads, the money we spend, the wisdom and knowledge we are blessed with that helps us to prosper, the cars we drive, our education, our careers and jobs, our businesses, our children, and the list goes on and on are all gifts from our LORD God almighty.

When we think about the kindness and generosity of our Father in Heaven towards us in creating us in the first instance and giving us breath (*Genesis 2: 7*), which is then topped up by giving us His one and only begotten Son, our Lord Jesus Christ (*John 3:16*), to die for our sins and shed his blood for our salvation at calvary. As if that was not enough, He then gives us His Holy Spirit when we obey his teachings and commands (*Acts 5: 32*).

*16For God so loved the world that **he gave his one and only Son**, that whoever believes in him shall not perish but have eternal life. 17For God did* *not send His Son into the world to condemn the world, but to save the world through him.*

John 3:16-17

What more could we have asked for from our Father in Heaven that we have not already received. Nothing, which is why thanksgiving is key for every believer to indulge in and express on a regular basis because all of us, the creation of our LORD God almighty have been immensely and generously blessed in a manner that has allowed us not to lack anything.

One then asks the question, why do we always appear not to be satisfied with the blessings and the gifts that we receive from our Father in Heaven. What readily comes to mind is **our lack of contentment** and it explains why Paul wrote in his letter to Timothy in *1 Timothy 6: 8* that godliness with contentment is great gain. It is something that we should embrace wholeheartedly and without any hesitation or equivocation as we progress on a daily basis in our Christian walk.

*6But **godliness with contentment** is great gain. 7For we brought nothing into the world, and we can take nothing out of it. 8But if we have food and clothing, we will be content with that. 9**Those who want to get rich** fall into temptation and a trap and into many foolish and harmful desires that plunge people into ruin and destruction. 10For **the love of money is a root of all kinds of evil**. Some people, eager for money, have wandered from the faith and pierced themselves with many griefs. 11**But you, man of God, flee from all this, and pursue righteousness, godliness, faith, love, endurance and gentleness**. 12Fight the good fight of the faith. Take hold of the eternal life to which you were called when you made your good confession in the presence of many witnesses.*

1 Timothy 6: 6-12

CHAPTER 17

The Majesty of God

I have chosen **Psalm 104** in almost its entirety to espouse the Majesty of our LORD God almighty and thereafter the eulogy of Paul in **Romans 8:31-39**. Please take your time to read it carefully and reflect on each word as it illuminates your mind with His incomprehensible and incomparable nature, which is beyond majestic greatness and as such impossible to be captured or described with words alone.

I pray that each word blesses you as your read on.

¹Let all that I am praise the LORD.

O LORD my God, how great You are! You are robed with honour and majesty.

²You are dressed in a robe of light. You stretch out the starry curtain of the heavens;

³You lay out the rafters of Your home in the rain clouds. You make the clouds Your chariot; You ride upon the wings of the wind.

⁴The winds are Your messengers; flames of fire are Your servants.

⁵You placed the world on its foundation so it would never be moved.

⁶You clothed the earth with floods of water, water that covered even the mountains.

⁷At Your command, the waters fled; at the sound of Your thunder, it hurried away.

⁸Mountains rose and valleys sank to the levels You decreed.

⁹Then You set a firm boundary for the seas, so they would never again cover the earth.

¹⁰*You make springs pour water into the ravines, so streams gush down from the mountains.*

¹¹*They provide water for all the animals, and the wild donkeys quench their thirst.*

¹²*The birds nest beside the streams and sing among the branches of the trees.*

¹³*You send rain on the mountains from Your heavenly home, and You fill the earth with the fruit of Your labour.*

¹⁴*You cause grass to grow for the livestock and plants for people to use. You allow them to produce food from the earth—*

¹⁵*wine to make them glad, olive oil to soothe their skin, and bread to give them strength.*

¹⁶*The trees of the LORD are well cared for—the cedars of Lebanon that He planted.*

¹⁷*There the birds make their nests, and the storks make their homes in the cypresses.*

¹⁸*High in the mountains live the wild goats, and the rocks form a refuge for the hyraxes.*

¹⁹*You made the moon to mark the seasons, and the sun knows when to set.*

²⁰*You send the darkness, and it becomes night, when all the forest animals prowl about.*

²¹*Then the young lions roar for their prey, stalking the food provided by God.*

²²*At dawn they slink back into their dens to rest.*

²³*Then people go off to their work, where they labour until evening.*

²⁴*O Lord, what a variety of things You have made! In wisdom You have made them all. The earth is full of Your creatures.*

²⁵*Here is the ocean, vast and wide, teeming with life of every kind, both large and small.*

²⁶*See the ships sailing along, and Leviathan, which You made to play in the sea.*

27They all depend on You to give them food as they need it.

28When You supply it, they gather it. You open Your hand to feed them, and they are richly satisfied.

29But if You turn away from them, they panic. When You take away their breath, they die and turn again to dust.

30When You give them Your breath, life is created, and You renew the face of the earth.

31May the glory of the LORD continue forever! The LORD takes pleasure in all He has made!

32The earth trembles at His glance; the mountains smoke at His touch.

33I will sing to the LORD as long as I live. I will praise my God to my last breath!

34May all my thoughts be pleasing to Him, for I rejoice in the LORD.

35Let all that I am praise the LORD. Praise the LORD!

Psalms 104: 1-35 (NLT)

Epilogue

After all said and done, from my personal experience, I can say categorically that the Christian walk is not a bed of roses and neither is it a walk in the park. The indwelling presence and empowerment of the Holy Spirit is required in order to live it to the full.

Some of us were born into Christian homes and we make the decision to remain in faith throughout our lives, irrespective of the challenges we face on the journey of life. Others are attracted to it from other faiths and religions as well as those with no faith at all, because of the message of salvation and eternal life with our Lord Jesus Christ when our time on earth ends. Still others who were born into the Christian faith rejected it because they simply could not relate to it for all kinds of reasons, which include the many challenges that Christians face in their journey of life. It is thus imperative that we are not ignorant in that we should know what we are up against.

*[10]Finally, be strong in the Lord and in his mighty power. [11]**Put on the full armour of God**, so that you can take your stand against the devil's schemes. [12]For our struggle is not against flesh and blood, but against the rulers, against the authorities, against the powers of this dark world and against the spiritual forces of evil in the heavenly realms. [13]Therefore put on **the full armour of God,** so that when the day of evil comes, you may be able to stand your ground, and after you have done everything, to stand. [14]Stand firm then, with **the belt of truth buckled** around your waist, with **the breastplate of righteousness in place,** [15]and with your **feet fitted** with the readiness that comes from **the gospel of peace**. [16]In addition to all this, **take up the shield of faith**, with which you can extinguish all the flaming arrows of the evil one. [17]**Take the helmet of salvation** and **the sword of the Spirit,** which is the word of God. [18]And **pray in the Spirit** on all occasions with all*

kinds of prayers and requests. With this in mind, be alert and always keep on praying for all the saints.

Ephesians 6:10-18

It is enough to say that the Christian walk is still the ultimate big deal. Once you grasp it, particularly with the help of the Holy Spirit, everything else pales into insignificance, as it ushers in the Kingdom of Heaven on earth experience, which has already been explained in several of the chapters in this book.

It is a different life that cannot easily be explained to the uninitiated. **As it is often said - the proof of the pudding is in the eating.** Once you have experienced what it means to live a life that is truly yielded, filled and empowered by the Holy Spirit, what else then is out there for you to seek or pursue? In my view, it is the ultimate experience of Kingdom living on this side of eternity.

That said, our decision to receive our Lord Jesus Christ and believe in him as our Lord and Savior, must not be for any other reason apart from for the reason of salvation, sanctification and eternal life with our LORD God almighty, otherwise the expectations from our Christian walk could easily become carnal and if we are not careful, we run the risk of losing our focus on the essence of obedience, holiness and righteousness, which attracts all the other blessings that our Lord Jesus Christ promised would be given to us as well (***Matthew 6:33***).

It is something that we have to be aware of and as such do everything to avoid. Yes, whether or not we receive our miracles and likewise, whether or not we enjoy all the breakthroughs that we prayed for, our LORD God almighty remains on the throne. On our part, **we remain more than conquerors.**

We Are More than Conquerors

³¹What, then, shall we say in response to these things? If God is for us, who can be against us? ³²He who did not spare his own Son, but gave him up for us all—how will he not also, along with him, graciously give us all things? ³³Who will bring any charge against those whom God has chosen? It is God who justifies. ³⁴Who then is the one who condemns? No one. Christ Jesus who died—more than that, who was raised to life—is at the right hand of God and is also interceding for us. **³⁵Who shall separate us from the love of Christ? Shall trouble or hardship or persecution or famine or nakedness or danger or sword?** *³⁶As it is written: "For your sake we face death all day long; we are considered as sheep to be slaughtered."* **³⁷No, in all these things we are more than conquerors through him who loved us. ³⁸For I am convinced that neither death nor life, neither angels nor demons, neither the present nor the future, nor any powers, ³⁹neither height nor depth, nor anything else in all creation, will be able to separate us from the love of God that is in Christ Jesus our Lord.**

Romans 8: 31-39

OPPORTUNITY TO BLESS OTHERS

If you have enjoyed reading **FATHER, I NEED HELP** and it has impacted your life in a positive way. Why not take the step to bless others with a copy or more of the book. You may wish to bless your friends, family member, church small groups, classmates, or even your work colleagues.

Copies of the book are available on Amazon. You can also order bulk purchases directly at a discount from the website of HFC Publications Limited – www.hfcpublications.com or you can reach out to a member of our team at books@hfcpublications.com.

Thank you.

ABOUT THE AUTHOR

First and foremost, Bola regards himself as a friend and servant of our Lord Jesus Christ. He is a non-practicing Solicitor of England and Wales, an Educationist, Businessman, Speaker, Writer, and Mentor to many people across many fields and denominations in different parts of the world. Bola is also the Lead Servant of Heritage Foundation for Christ. A not-for-profit Christian organization. Bola is married with two grown-up children and lives in London, United Kingdom.

BOLA MAKINDE